THE COVERT CODE

ANNA COVERT

THE

COVERT

CODE

MASTERING
THE ART
OF DIGITAL
MARKETING

Forbes | Books

Published by Forbes Books, Charleston, South Carolina.
An imprint of Advantage Media Group.

Forbes Books is a registered trademark, and the Forbes Books colophon is a trademark of Forbes Media, LLC.

Printed in the United States of America.

10 9 8 7 6 5 4 3 2 1

ISBN: 979-8-88750-497-1 (Hardcover)
ISBN: 979-8-88750-608-1 (Paperback)
ISBN: 979-8-88750-498-8 (eBook)

Library of Congress Control Number: 2024903672

Cover design by Analisa Smith.
Layout design by Matthew Morse.

This custom publication is intended to provide accurate information and the opinions of the author in regard to the subject matter covered. It is sold with the understanding that the publisher, Forbes Books, is not engaged in rendering legal, financial, or professional services of any kind. If legal advice or other expert assistance is required, the reader is advised to seek the services of a competent professional.

Since 1917, Forbes has remained steadfast in its mission to serve as the defining voice of entrepreneurial capitalism. Forbes Books, launched in 2016 through a partnership with Advantage Media, furthers that aim by helping business and thought leaders bring their stories, passion, and knowledge to the forefront in custom books. Opinions expressed by Forbes Books authors are their own. To be considered for publication, please visit **books.Forbes.com**.

This book is dedicated to my mother who is my best friend and biggest fan. Growing up dyslexic was tough, but with her love and support I never let it hold me back. She always told me never to compare myself to other people and taught me that I could become whatever I dreamed... Thanks for always believing in me, Mom. I love you!

1000011 01101111 01100100 01100101 00100000 01001101 01100001 0111
1110010 01101001 01101110 01100111 00100000 01110100 01101000 0110
1110010 01110100 00100000 01101111 01100110 00100000 01000100 0110
1110100 01100001 01101100 00100000 01001101 01100001 01110010 0110
1101001 01101110 01100111 01010100 01101000 01100101 00100000 0100
1100101 01110010 01110100 00100000 01000011 01101111 01100100 0110
1100001 01110011 01110100 01100101 01110010 01101001 01101110 0110
1101000 01100101 00100000 01000001 01110010 01110100 00100000 0110
1000100 01101001 01100111 01101001 01110100 01100001 01101100 0010
1110010 01101011 01100101 01110100 01101001 01101110 01100111 0101
0100000 01000011 01101111 01110110 01100101 01110010 01110100 0010
1100100 01100101 00100000 01001101 01100001 01110011 01110100 0110
1101110 01100111 00100000 01110100 01101000 01100101 00100000 0100
0100000 01101111 01100110 00100000 01000100 01101001 01100111 0110
1101100 00100000 01001101 01100001 01110010 01101011 01100101 0111
1100111 01010100 01101000 01100101 00100000 01000011 01101111 0111
1110100 00100000 01000011 01101111 01100100 01100101 00100000 0100
1110100 01100101 01110010 01101001 01101110 01100111 00100000 0111
0100000 01000001 01110010 01110100 00100000 01101111 01100110 0010
1100111 01101001 01110100 01100001 01101100 00100000 01001101 0110
1100101 01110100 01101001 01101110 01100111 01010100 01101000 0110
1101111 01110110 01100101 01110010 01110100 00100000 01000011 0110
0100000 01001101 01100001 01110011 01110100 01100101 01110010 0110
0100000 01110100 01101000 01100101 00100000 01000001 01110010 0111
1100110 00100000 01000100 01101001 01100111 01101001 01110100 0110
1001101 01100001 01110010 01101011 01100101 01110100 01101001 0110
1101000 01100101 00100000 01000011 01101111 01110110 01100101 0111
1000011 01101111 01100100 01100101 00100000 01001101 01100001 0111
1110010 01101001 01101110 01100111 00100000 01110100 01101000 0110
1110010 01110100 00100000 01101111 01100110 00100000 01000100 0110
1110100 01100001 01101100 00100000 01001101 01100001 01110010 0110
1101001 01101110 01100111 01010100 01101000 01100101 00100000 0100
1100101 01110010 01110100 00100000 01000011 01101111 01100100 0110
1100001 01110011 01110100 01100101 01110010 01101001 01101110 0110
1101000 01100101 00100000 01000001 01110010 01110100 00100000 0110
1000100 01101001 01100111 01101001 01110100 01100001 01101100 0010
1110010 01101011 01100101 01110100 01101001 01101110 01100111 0101
0100000 01000011 01101111 01110110 01100101 01110010 01110100 0010
1100100 01100101 00100000 01001101 01100001 01110011 01110100 0110
1101110 01100111 00100000 01110100 01101000 01100101 00100000 0100
0100000 01101111 01100110 00100000 01000100 01101001 01100111 0110
1101100 00100000 01001101 01100001 01110010 01101011 01100101 0111
1100111 01010100 01101000 01100101 00100000 01000011 01101111 0111
1110100 00100000 01000011 01101111 01100100 01100101 00100000 0100
1110100 01100101 01110010 01101001 01101110 01100111 00100000 0111
0100000 01000001 01110010 01110100 00100000 01101111 01100110 0010

01000011 0110111
01101111 01100100 01100101 0010000
0010000
01101111 0110011
01101111 01100100 0110010
01101111 0110011
01101111 01100110 00100000

CONTENTS

01000011 0110111
01101111 01100100 01100101 0010000
0010000
01101111 0110011
01101111 01100100 0110010
01101111 0110011
01101111 01100110 00100000

ABOUT
THE
AUTHOR

Anna Covert is the founder of Covert Communication, the largest digital marketing firm in Hawaii. Over the past twenty years, she has become recognized in the industry as an authority in digital advertising and is known for her unwavering business ethics. A powerhouse, Covert has worked with hundreds of companies worldwide, in a wide range of industries. Her team has developed API technology solutions for both SunPower and Panasonic, and is featured as a preferred marketing partner for their extensive dealer networks.

From high-end consulting with Fortune 500 companies to helping small businesses avoid being taken advantage of, her mission is to uplift the industry and protect consumers from the escalating online marketing and media fraud that plagues online platforms, including Search, Display, and other online advertising platforms and networks. A true entrepreneur, Covert also operates several other marketing and technology businesses including reactium.io, which is currently being used by enterprise organizations worldwide with contributors from Apple, Microsoft, and IBM.

Anna graduated cum laude from Bentley University—Business School in Waltham, Massachusetts with a Bachelor of Science in Marketing and a minor in Management. In her spare time, she enjoys golf, travel, and spending time in the orchid house with her daughter.

01000011 0110111
01101111 01100100 01100101 0010000
0010000
01101111 0110011
01101111 01100100 0110010
01101111 0110011
01101111 01100110 00100000

INTRODUCTION

To win a game, you need to know two things: the rules and how to read a crowd. From pool to poker, mahjong to marbles, the rules of the game don't change, but your environment does. The winners can sense changes and adjust their strategy in real time, allowing them to gain a significant advantage over their competitors.

The same is true when you buy and sell online media. Unlike traditional marketing, the ad exchange is happening in real time as a live auction. It's like the stock exchange, but it never sleeps. Consumers are on their devices, engaging with ads and content, 24/7. So many things affect your bidding and buying strategy online—seasonality, competitiveness, sociocultural issues, and even weather impact a company's results and overall marketing spend.

When you buy traditional ads, the price is fixed, and after the media negotiation takes place, the final price-per-spot, page, column, card, etc. are agreed upon, and an IO (insertion order) is created, locking in the rate. Then, you trust that the projected impressions you were promised will be delivered. On the other hand, if you work with a big media buyer who uses comprehensive software that proves that the expected or promised TRPs (total rating points) from a spot aired during a broadcast show did not occur, a credit may be issued.

Generally, there isn't a refund, but the advertiser may get "make good" ads to ensure that your brand achieves the reach that was paid for.

I remember working at my first agency and attending the annual "sweep" screenings with our media director to preview all the new shows airing that season. Each network came out with a list, and those shows with projected high popularity would command premium rates. Sometimes the networks were right, but many times they were wrong, and the show would fail to perform as projected. Nevertheless, if the network guessed incorrectly, at the end of the season, we would tally up the delivered TRPs, and then the network would run extra spots to "make good" on the promised impressions. These are estimates, of course, and were based on the number of TVs that are on or "tuned in," but they didn't account for when grandpa slept through the commercials or when someone forgot to turn off the TV. That wasn't the fault of the network or station. And it was fair. It was also something they could prove. For example, if we had any doubt that our spot aired on the day and time promised, we could request a report from Nielsen. They record every station nationwide and can pull a copy of your TV spot. Scarborough does this for radio, and there are companies that audit print publications for distribution to make sure that copies of magazines or newspapers are delivered. There are even organizations that hire people to stand on the side of the road and click the number of cars that drive past billboards to assure advertisers that the promised results are delivered. You get the idea.

Now, what if I told you that there is no third-party oversight for online advertising?

That's right, there is no way to prove, using an unbiased entity, that your ad or impression ever ran. That should scare you. That's why picking the right partners and asking the right questions are critical. Business owners must stop believing in the promise of "guilty until proven innocent," and instead assume the worst when it comes to buying media online. Your partner *must* prove themselves worthy of your trust.

Sadly, many agencies and media partners are not honest. I don't believe this is universally a grand scheme to hurt business owners, but rather it's the result of a total lack of industry knowledge that has trickled down and tarnished the industry. Digital marketing didn't become a dark art by itself; it has become that way from years of rapid and untamed growth.

But the good news is that business owners can master the art of online marketing and take back control by learning the fundamentals of how media is bought, sold, and consumed online. This book will uncover the "game" and arm you with *Covert Code* strategies that will prepare you to fight the battle today and win the war for years to come. From picking the right partner to knowing when it's time to push the brakes and regroup on your digital strategy, you can and will be able to target the right people, with the right message, at the right time, achieving your desired ROI without the aid of a big agency or high media spend.

Why am I so confident? Because I have done it for myself over the last twenty years and, in the process, built Covert Communication, the largest digital marketing firm in Hawaii. I've worked with clients of all shapes and sizes, helping them to achieve their business goals. Although my agency specializes in digital marketing, we're full-service and my team has a rich background in traditional media buying, breakout public relations, creative production, website and application development, email marketing, social media, sales funnels, and branding. We've done it all and have leveraged our deep knowledge of foundational advertising from both client and agency perspectives to drive exceptional online results, earning the reputation as a leader in digital marketing while providing transparent media solutions that work.

Since 2019, we have worked with hundreds of companies worldwide, with a focus on SunPower and Panasonic solar companies and manufacturers developing API technology solutions. We're featured as preferred marketing partners for their extensive dealer networks. In addition to the solar space, we have worked in hospitality, banking, real estate, retail, insurance, travel and tourism, transportation, technology…. The list is long. We've been hired to provide high-end consulting for Fortune 500 companies, because time and time again, our marketing solutions work better than the rest. Covert is so bold that we will even guarantee clients that, by spending their current budget and using our strategies, they will experience a minimum 20 percent increase in results.

It's not magic. It's math mixed with a pinch of persistence, and any business owner can replicate those results by following *The Covert Code*. Our clients not only spend less out of the gate but, over time, have doubled and tripled their revenue year-over-year, resulting in more agency referrals and business than we can accept. Our model is unique in that we don't believe in media commission. When we do our job right, through robust and thoughtful online optimization, clients spend less, not more, making the traditional model of compensation archaic. We believe in transparency and sharing knowledge, numbers, and strategies. Our clients view us as part of their internal team. That's how it should be. They can trust us because our interests are aligned and anything we recommend is because we believe it will make more money, not because we're taking a cut. As a result, every day the emails and calls flood in with client referrals and Zoom meetings filled with celebrations of milestones achieved.

That's precisely why I knew that now was the time to write this book and share my knowledge with the business community at scale.

The truth is that today it's rare that a company would have no experience with online advertising. Even the smallest mom & pop business has a Squarespace/Wix/GoDaddy website and has listed an enhanced profile Yellow Pages map ad, purchased a search engine optimization (SEO) package, or tried to boost a Facebook post. I speak with clients every day, and it doesn't matter their size, industry, or budget, the story is the same. By the time they've reached me, they've already been through three or more agencies, spending hundreds of thousands of dollars online, and without the promised result.

I'm tired of hearing the sad stories and outrage from hardworking business owners who are just trying their best and can't afford to place trust in all the wrong places. My clients have been victims of digital marketing fraud in all forms, across all networks—Google, Microsoft, Facebook, Geofencing, Yelp, SEO, the list is long. My agency has been a victim, too. The result? I know how to spot a fraud and win online. I believe that, by writing *The Covert Code* and sharing my experiences while learning these tools, I'll be able to prevent business owners like you from being taken for a ride. I want to help you win online.

We'll begin by learning the basics of how media is consumed online and options for reaching the right target audience through networks, ad types, and bidding strategies. Then, we'll identify our customers' online journey and how to set the correct online budget and project results from your campaigns. As you build knowledge in each chapter, we'll shift the focus to core elements of your media strategy and learn how to drive traffic to your site from both paid and organic sources, as well as to ensure that every dollar spent has the greatest opportunity to convert. We'll dive deep into remarketing, SEO, bots, paid search, and social media. Each section you'll find cheat sheets online to help you get control of your campaigns immediately and start improving results in real time. For those readers who really want to "get their geek on," additional breakout content and online quizzes are available to ensure that you've mastered the code chapter by chapter. To maximize your results and achieve immediate value, it's recommended that you gain access to all of your accounts using the "getting started" reference guide and also print out "Anna's tips," which will appear in each chapter.

Lastly, as things happen fast online, please be sure to subscribe to our newsletter so you can be notified of any new cheat sheets or updates from the Covert team on campaign settings that offer opportunities or threats to your online performance. Now, take a deep breath and have fun unlocking the code!

01000011 011011
01101111 01100100 01100101 0010000
0010000
01101111 011001
01101111 01100100 0110001
01101111 011001
01101111 01100110 00100000

CHAPTER ONE

THE RULES FOR DIGITAL MEDIA

My journey in business started at Bentley College in 2001–2004 (yes, I graduated early), where I learned about traditional marketing, management, finance, accounting, economics, philosophy, and next to nothing about technology. In fact, there wasn't even a chapter on digital marketing in Advertising 1.0. It was all about the purchase funnel and how to move the customer through, via push or pull marketing strategies using the 4 P's: Product, Price, Place, and Promotion. Websites were used as digital brochures, just a static way for companies to connect with customers who already knew them, and were purely to establish credibility. Even today, as digital media becomes the most critical part of the media mix, the mothership of all brand communication, it is still a mystery to most and thus offers the greatest opportunity for businesses to meet and exceed sales goals through optimization.

The fundamentals of advertising haven't changed. What has are how the 4 P's are deployed and which media tools should be used to influence customer action.

It's for this reason that I always begin every new client meeting, public speaking engagement, or corporate training session with a big picture of the purchase funnel. For those who have never had the opportunity to work with an advertising agency during the initial discovery call, I go through a pitch that goes a little something like depicted in the graphic here.

Our job as marketers is to move our target audience or customer from the top of the funnel to the bottom through the four stages: Awareness, Consideration, Intent, and Action.

At each level of the funnel, we use different marketing tactics and media to influence our target audience. Each stage of the funnel comes with expectations of results and will vary by media type. In traditional advertising, there is an equation for how to reach what we refer to as "critical mass." Essentially, marketing is a math problem and we know that we need to target 98 percent of our target audience with four to seven messages over seven to ten days, and if we do that, we will get a 2 percent conversion. Here's an example: you have heard about the McRib from McDonald's, right? Every year, this popular product comes back for a limited-time, one-month-long promo. You might ask yourself why would McDonald's spend all that money on something that is only in-store for one month? Their goal is to steal market share from similar quick-service competitors like Burger King, Carl's Jr., etc. They hope (and have data to back it up) that, for whatever reason, they can influence a consumer's long-term behavior. As an example: Joe goes to Burger King loyally several times a week for a burger and shake, but this week he decides to go to McDonald's to get the McRib during the limited promotional window. When he does, for whatever reason, this cosmic shift occurs that changes his meal-buying pattern *forever*. Maybe McDonald's is a faster drive from his house or the parking is easier, maybe he has a crush on the cashier serving his meal. Whatever the reason, the result is that he switches loyalty and continues to go to McDonald's, even after the promotion ends, to purchase his regular burger and shake. As McDonald's knows about Critical Mass Messaging, they are not going to wait seven to ten days to show the required four to seven ads (impressions) because then they only have two more weeks left in the promotional calendar (and, for the record, they run way more than seven ads). Instead, they jam as many TV commercials as they can into the first five days and then extend it over the following promotional period with a combination of fifteen-second TV bookends and radio with supporting print. They always start with TV because when the customer hears the ad later on radio or sees a print ad, they rerun the TV spot in their minds, which essentially extends the brand impact—more bang for your bucks!

That is why you might see several commercials back-to-back. The human brain needs multiple reminders to move us from the top of the purchase funnel to the bottom. The more we see the same thing, the faster we move from awareness to action. That is true for all media types, traditional to digital. So, in our example, if we were selling McRibs in Hawaii, our target audience would be adults over the age of eighteen, or roughly one million people. We expect that around 70 percent slip into consideration—"Oh boy, it's back, I might want to go." Of that, 30 percent make it to intent—"Where is the closest store to me, and what day works for my schedule?" Finally a minimum of 2 percent (approximately 22,000 people) will actually get to the counter and buy the promotional item.

It worked in the past and still does. The problem has always been that mass marketing is expensive and hard to track. To quote that famous retail magnate John Wanamaker, "Half the money I spend on advertising is wasted; the trouble is I don't know which half." And it really isn't fair to small companies that can't afford to spend money and hope that the person who needs whatever they're selling happens to stumble upon their quarter-page ad and act. Traditional marketing is semi-targeted and an expensive luxury afforded to the bigger and more established companies that can afford to waste funds. This old way of advertising creates more significant barriers to entry, making it hard for entrepreneurs without deep pockets to succeed. Just because you can overspend doesn't mean you should. That being said, we know that traditional marketing does work if you do it right and will always have an important place in the media mix. The part that is lost to most is "How exactly do you effectively buy media online," which is why you're reading this book. So, let's start with the basic concepts, and then we'll go into each tool in detail.

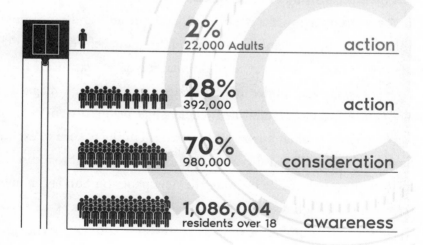

Impact Of Critical Mass Messaging

2%
22,000 Adults — action

28%
392,000 — action

70%
980,000 — consideration

1,086,004
residents over 18 — awareness

THE AD EXCHANGE EXPLAINED

When I first got my toes wet in an online search over a decade ago, there weren't many options. Google basically had a monopoly and dominated the "ad exchange," and still does to a large extent, which is the current subject of several lawsuits[1] (do a quick search of "google lawsuits" to learn more). But what, pray tell, is the ad exchange? An ad exchange is an online marketplace where advertisers buy digital ad inventory from publishers, often through real-time bidding (RTB) auctions. An ad space could be inventory on a website or mobile app, or seconds of air time during a podcast or video stream. Typically any website that has over 10,000 unique daily visitors can qualify to participate as a seller and be collectively referred to as a publisher. That means that they can open inventory up on their website pages (domain URL, app, video streaming service, social media platform) and then get paid by offering those spaces to advertisers to fill gaps in the content (banner ads, text ads, content ads, and video ads). This was a big deal when it first came out because, before that, digital ads were sold the same way as traditional media. It was the "*build it and they will come*" model. Media companies like CNN, magazines like *People*, and large established retailers like Walmart went to their existing network of ad buyers and offered them the chance to extend their reach by adding a digital package to their print, broadcast, or in-store promo. Just like opening the newspaper on Sunday, as subscribers or loyal followers went to the site, your company's ad would show a specific number of times, that is, impressions. It seems reasonable right? Well sure, if you want to spend more than you must.

---

1   "Justice department sues Google for monopolizing digital advertising technologies," Office of Public Affairs, Department of Justice, January 24, 2023, https://www.justice.gov/opa/pr/justice-department-sues-google-monopolizing-digital-advertising-technologies.

Now, let's identify all the various ways that media can be bought and consumed online today, starting with networks and content types.

BANNER ADS

These are the most common online content types available. Today, there are thirty-five sizes that banner ads can be formatted to maximize a business's opportunity to be seen across web and mobile display. We'll talk more about why this matters in chapter 8, when we dive into remarketing, or as I lovingly refer to it, "cyber-stalking." Banner ads can be static, animated (my personal favorite), video, or dynamic, which is most commonly used for retailers or real estate companies that have product catalogs of some kind. This type of display ad is more tailored because it can show specific items to your target audience based on their browsing or search behavior, that is, you see the same products you added to your shopping cart or viewed during your recent visit. Static ads and animated ads can be formatted several ways but must remain between 150 and 500 kb and load within thirty seconds, with loop or without, and available sizes vary by your media distribution partner. Recently, some media publishers like Criteo, Quancast, and StackAdapt have even opened up selected video banner ads in three sizes—horizontal, vertical, and square (thirty seconds)—offering advertisers even more opportunity to engage with customers on the page using sight, sound, and motion.

NATIVE ADS

These are often referred to as "click bait" and disguise themselves as article content. They use a combination of a text headline and image with the goal to increase website traffic to learn more, and can be very effective to generate clicks. However, they often result in high bounce rates (which means that the customer got to your site but then left immediately). This can inflate the cost of your campaign and be ineffective without a remarketing campaign and clear key performance indicator (KPI) goals in place, which we will review in chapter 8.

PRE-ROLL VIDEO

These are like a traditional TV commercial but run online before other video content rolls. For example, if you go to a news site and want to watch a debate or other content, a pre-roll video commercial may run before the user has the opportunity to watch the free content from that publisher. Pre-roll video is most commonly fifteen seconds, thirty seconds, or sixty seconds in length. For some publishers like YouTube, the customer can choose to "skip" the ad after seven seconds. It is for this reason that I do not recommend using a publisher with skip options, but for those who wish to run ads on YouTube, make sure that your logo and CTA (call to action) are in the front of your ad versus the end, to maximize brand value and impression share.

TEXT ADS

These ads are just as you'd expect and contain a text headline (up to three lines) and then one or two lines of description copy. They are the most ineffective form of online advertising when used *outside* of a search engine network. We'll dive deeper into that when we get to our chapter 7 on search engine marketing (SEM).

To distribute ads online you must use a publisher that offers various options for targeting:

Display Advertising

Ads are shown on URLs that qualify to be on the ad exchange in the form of any banner ad, pre-roll video, or native ad. Whenever an ad is displayed, the URL (such as yahoo.com) will be paid by the publisher for impressions displayed. You can easily identify if the content is being delivered by a media publisher because, on the top right corner, you will see a tiny blue cone and, if you hover over it, it will show you advertising preference and which publisher is distributing the content, that is, AdSense, Criteo, AdRoll, StackAdapt, Quantcast, etc. If you do not see the cone, it means that the ad was purchased directly by the advertiser with the website owner. This happens frequently on news sites when advertisers extend their traditional advertising campaign online.

Native Ads/Pre-roll Video

Native ads and pre-roll videos run on the display network and appear as featured content inside of the main URL's or app's content. You can identify them by looking at the subject line above the block of ads, which will say "paid partner content." You pay for the impressions served and the prices will vary depending on the site that the ad runs on.

Search Network

Search ads appear inside of the search engine's landing page (Google. com, Bing.com, etc.) and are purchased by the advertiser directly with the search engine or their ad exchange partner.

 ANNA'S TIP

Search ads that appear within Google or Bing are essentially free to the platform. They have an opportunity cost versus hard cost.

Partner Networks

Partner networks are essentially the way that search engines increase reach by serving text ads outside of their domain. Ads can appear above or below search results on Google/Microsoft Search. They can appear next to, above, or below search results on the Shopping tab, Images, Maps, and the Maps app. So, if you allow your text ads to be shown across the partner network in GoogleAds, your text ad could be shown across hundreds of non-Google websites but no clear list is provided (the same is true for Microsoft). This is very ineffective overall and increases the advertiser's total cost exponentially, as there is no way to block bots outside of the search engine.

Programmatic Advertising

Programmatic advertising offers an alternative to traditional trading desk distribution (single-channel media partner inventory) and is referred to as a DSP or Demand-Side Platform. DSPs are AI-driven, digital marketing platforms that reach new markets, audiences, and channels and are bid on in real time in a live media auction by advertisers. We can use these platforms to reach users cross-device, worldwide, with Display, Native, Video, Audio (Webs Streaming, Digital Radio, Podcasts), Connected TV (CTV) Advertising, In-Game, and Digital Out-Of-Home (DOOH) based on our target's geography, audience demographics, interests, and 1st-party/3rd-party data, and can access inventory across multiple media publishers in real time.

DOOH

DOOH is any digital advertising that is found outside of the home, and in a public environment. This fairly new form of media can be integrated with programmatic technology to automate the buying, selling, and display of ads on selected screens in venues like bus stops, airport displays, shopping mall displays, gas stations, gyms, movie theaters, office buildings, residential buildings, restaurants and bars, retail locations, street furniture, transit, universities, convenience stores, and even city squares. The types of ads that can run on DOOH include static, dynamic, video, and even interactive experiences. The way that media partners charge is based on what is called the Impression Multiplier or a one-to-many channel type. Impression multiples are third-party audited by premium geolocation and device ID vendors. Advertisers can purchase ads based on a loop or static inventory.

There are three types of common DOOH inventory types:

- *Large format*—billboards to bus shelters, best viewed by pedestrians and street foot traffic.
- *Place based*—located in contextually relevant environments like gas stations, taxis, restaurants, and others.
- *Point-of-purchase*—which is considered a subcategory of place-based inventory and happens within point-of-purchase signage in retail locations that influence action in store. These are like traditional "shelf talkers," but are animated and controlled digitally.

In-Game Advertising

Blended In-Game advertising allows companies to reach a highly engaged audience at scale. Blended In-Game ads are available in display and video formats and can be targeted based on geography, third-party audiences, custom segments, look-alike audiences, and retargeting audiences. How does it work? Based on the type of customer you are trying to reach, you can select gaming networks to show your ad over desktop/laptops, tablets, mobile devices, and consoles like Xbox along with a variety of other publishers. The benefits of In-Game advertising are that with this non-distributive messaging the user is captivated and unlikely to be multitasking. In-Gaming can reach a global audience with access to players in North America, EMEA, and APAC. As there is no "click" ability, it's no surprise that the only way to bid is by impression or CPM. Companies like StackAdapt allow programmatic reach through the open exchange and PMP deals, allowing companies to bid for impression share with control and narrow in on gamers across all genres, that is, Action, Adventure, Casual, Sports, Racing, Role-Playing, and more! One of the most exciting parts about this new advertising type is that it's private and safe following compliance standards.[2] Plus, unlike with so many media publishers, the invalid traffic (IVT) rate is <1 percent, which confirms that the impressions were seen by real people (not automated software, a.k.a. bots) across all formats. Yes reader, this means you can trust what you purchase!

These formats use Automated Aspect Ratio Matching, meaning the ad will render to match the environment where the ad is appearing and can include display ads or video ads. In terms of trackable metrics, we can see impressions, unique impressions, viewability rate, video completion rate, IVT rate, and domain and game name where the ad was served.

PROGRAMMATIC AUDIO

Programmatic audio is the ability to target via audio ads and is billed by CMP (typical pricing starts around $15), but advertisers can evaluate campaign effectiveness from the Cost-per-Completed-Listen (eCPCL). Delivery options include inventory of fifteen- or thirty-second spots. Advertisers can serve ads across three different types of listening content.

---

2   GDPR, CCPA, and COPPA compliance rules as well as ISO 27001 Information Security Standard Certified.

- *Music streaming*—Spotify, Pandora, or other streaming services and are automatically served an ad after listening.
- *Podcasts*—ads are inserted dynamically using RTB and ads play during a podcast sponsored slot.
- *Digital radio*—Same ad placements as traditional radio but ads are inserted dynamically using RTB online.

CONNECTED TV

This refers to the method by which most over-the-top (OTT) content is delivered to users beyond cable devices, that is, TV, mobile, tablet, apps, or desktop. CTV can connect to the internet and allow users to access their on-demand content, meaning your ad could appear on smart TVs, Apple TV, Roku, Amazon Fire Sticks, and gaming consoles like PlayStation and Xbox. Ads in this digital medium are billed by CPM (typical starting price $40 eCPM) and can be delivered in fifteen-, thirty-, or sixty-second varieties via MP4.

PRICING MODELS

Each media publisher has its own pricing model, but they boil down to three types of billing options: cost-per-thousand (CPM) impressions, cost-per-click (CPC), or cost-per-result (CPR), which can be further broken down by completed watch, listen, etc. Depending on where the ad runs and the type of content, the model and pricing vary. The most common pricing model is CPM, but this comes with more risks than rewards for business owners.

To add to the challenge of decoding all of these acronyms, CPM is sometimes referred to as eCPM, which means *estimated* CPM impressions. If you see the "e," that's good. It means that whatever exchange you're using is more transparent because, as we target users through the digital networks, the cost may vary from site-to-site or content-to-content type. For example, native ads or pre-roll video ads cost more than traditional display ads and the cost is also dependent on where they are shown. Depending on the publishing partner, the ranges can swing radically, but a good baseline for display CPM should be $3–$7. For native and pre-roll, a good target is $7–$20, and for DOOH ads, the range can vary drastically depending on location, time, and even weather. The more "weight" the company or venue has (or is perceived to have), the more they can charge. Golf.com charges more to run your thirty-second TV commercial before the clip showing Tiger Woods putting on the 18th green than Buzzfeed.com does before their videos. Why? Because that audience is worth more, or at least that's what they lead you to believe. I'm not saying they're wrong, but when we really expose CMP for what it is, it's just a view or single impression. The customer didn't click on it; they saw it for a few seconds (maybe).

The most important thing for a business owner is to target a customer that has interest in your product or service, but unless that customer acts, how do we quantify our media spend? And to say that the same user who watched your pre-roll video or experienced a display ad on golf.com is worth more than serving an ad to that same user on buzzfeed.com doesn't add up. An impression is an impression unless they act by clicking or visiting your site after being served an ad. Sadly, as there is no third-party non-biased oversight online to prove that an impression ran in the display network, this type of blind media spend isn't worth investing in for most companies unless you use a partner that will provide impression share and false/fake click reports. We'll dive deeper into this concept in chapter 3 when we uncover how your digital ads actually work and how to protect yourself.

CPC: COST-PER-CLICK

By far my favorite way to advertise online is CPC because it is the easiest to control and indicates that the target audience was interested and took action. The goal of online advertising is to drive valuable website traffic to your site, and a click is step one. The only gray area is who clicked on the ad (human versus bot) and were they someone we were trying to target, that is, in our geographic area matching desired demographic and psychographic attributes. The good news is that advertisers have some options to protect the integrity of their campaign using tools like ClickCease or partnering with companies like Criteo, StackAdapt, and Quantcast, who provide fraudulent click reports and third-party oversight. The bad news is that the biggest partners like Google, Microsoft, and Meta offer no protection inside of their platforms and advertisers are not able to use a third-party service to verify human versus bot clicks outside of the search network—partner, display networks, or YouTube. We'll dive deeper into how to protect your campaigns later in this book. For now, just know that CPC is the safest because we can use third-party software like Google Analytics to verify that users did arrive at our site from a specific URL or advertising campaign using Urchin Tracking Module (UTM) parameters (which you will learn how to set up in chapter 4). Then we can analyze that user's behavior to assess the value of the paid click, that is, did they stay/exit, did they buy/or what content did they interact with and how can you increase results to drive more conversions from your existing ad spend. The average CPC will vary dramatically by media distribution network ($0.15–$175+), which is why it's imperative to never let the media publisher "bid" on your behalf and never ever "set and forget" bid strategies.

CPA: COST-PER-ACTION

This bidding strategy is really what all business owners think they want, but it never seems to deliver. Essentially, a company agrees to an amount that they will pay the media publisher for every transaction generated by a paid ad campaign. For retailers, this is easier to quantify—yes, that human purchased something. But what it doesn't account for is the large swing in average cart price, or refunds. And for home services or most B2B companies, just because someone filled out a form on your website or made a call that lasted over sixty seconds does not mean that they became a customer. They might not have been qualified, the contact information might be incorrect, it could even have been a bot filling out your form. As a result, this is not a recommended way for business owners to buy ads online as it increases costs dramatically and reduces our ability to predict results from a planned marketing budget.

Now that we know the options for content types, pricing models, and distribution networks to deliver those ads, let's identify which media solutions work to target customers along the purchase funnel. Starting at the top of the funnel, the most effective tools to drive online awareness and consideration are using what we call Front-Funnel media solutions that target users based on behavioral and physiological attributes using programmatic targeting, that is, acquired datasets to determine the right audience and the best places to find them online and cross-network ad delivery. For most companies, these types of media buys are similar to a traditional media buy where you sign an IO and then the magic happens behind the scenes. Advertising agencies (like mine) are often granted "self-service" access that removes this high upfront cost for clients, allowing us to create, manage, and optimize campaigns without a contract or high minimum spend.

That being said, this access is not common and thus for companies with budgets starting at $5k per month to allocate toward *Awareness* advertising, companies like Quantcast and StackAdapt are recommended and a combination of native, pre-roll, and display advertising is utilized based on keywords, competitor sites, and other key metrics. For smaller ad buys, companies like Criteo and AdRoll offer ways to target users using look-alike or customer match lists.

The next funnel level, *Intent*, utilizes SEM and is the most effective way to generate trackable business because the user already knows what they are looking for and is actively on a search browser like Chrome, Firefox, Safari, or Edge, and seeking a solution using a keyword phrase. Some examples: two-bedroom condos near me, the best solar company, gluten-free cookies, etc.

Once the customer clicks on the ad and arrives at your website, *Action*, the next step in the funnel is to complete a transaction of some kind. Once the user does arrive at our domain, we attempt to "cookie" their IP address using a pixel that is placed on the header of every page of your website or within GoogleTagManager. Unless the customer has ad-blocking turned on, chooses to opt out of cookies, or visits your site using an incognito search, we will be able to target them in the future across digital networks (publishers) once they leave our website. We will also be able to create audience profiles of look-alike prospects that allow us to inform or create better seed lists for "top of the funnel" outreach. Remarketing is highly effective and a MUST-DO for any company engaging in paid advertising because, as you will recall, the human brain must see and experience your brand multiple times to influence action.

Although we have tools to reach customers along each phase of the purchase funnel, it's important to understand that they will not yield the same results as critical mass messaging. I remember years ago, when I was hired as an online media buyer by Doug Harris, the owner of the Harris Agency (my former employer before I started my own agency) to run a campaign for Jamba Juice, they were rolling out a special line of smoothies from a local celebrity chef. At the time media budgets were being cut across the board, as even big companies did not have the appetite to spend hundreds of thousands of dollars on traditional marketing. They were looking for ways to reduce costs and improve results through better targeting online. I created a program using the display and search network with a reputable partner to deliver the ads at every part of the funnel with a focus on awareness and consideration. The campaign launched, and the digital campaign was performing above expectations on impressions, clicks, and views. It was working by all measurable digital metrics. So I was surprised when Doug told me, "No one has seen the spots. When are we going to reach critical mass?" The answer was never. This was supposed to be an *extension* of the traditional media, not a replacement. When I realized they had changed the media mix, I reached out to my media partner to see if we could accelerate the ad delivery but, even then, it was never going to be fast enough to emulate traditional mass media. Why? Because it is just that: targeted not mass. Yes, the display ads were delivered to people who matched our audience types of those who drank smoothies and enjoyed *Top Chef.* But we were not able to deliver enough impressions over the promotional period to move the customer through the purchase funnel, and when they cut traditional reach too deeply, the result was unfavorable in comparison. Not only that, but the concept of changing behavior for those who were not already Jamba Juice lovers was missed. Like the McRib's example, our goal was to influence people who treated themselves to a snack of some kind. Not necessarily a smoothie, but something delicious, a Starbucks Mochaccino, a boba drink, something "like" but not an exact match to change behavior long term.

Digital is an extension of traditional and is used to reinforce a brand's credibility, but it can't create the same "urgency" as television or radio. An animated banner ad is a few seconds long and even if customers do watch our pre-roll video, did they make it to the end and are they going to watch it again to build up enough views to emulate critical mass messaging? The answer is usually "no." People get bored and skip when they can (exactly why I rarely spend clients' money on YouTube). Overall, the impact is not as deep. The consumer just doesn't feel the same pressure. The problem with trying to translate traditional media learning into digital is that it doesn't work the same way.

If we had ran that same campaign today, we would tackle the media mix differently and focus the front-funnel push on display ads and native ads that generate high-quality traffic with an irresistible offer versus a focus on watching a commercial, maybe a Free Snack with Smoothie Claim Coupon, and then focus the larger share of the budget on remarketing (Display and In-Game) with supporting pre-roll video, CTV, and digital audio to those same users. The results would change to align more with traditional critical mass goals to stimulate foot traffic, but instead of generating a 2 percent conversion of the audience, we would see that number jump up to 20–30 percent because we eliminated all of the waste that is inherited from traditional mass media and are now only focusing critical mass impression share on those users who indicate intent by clicking through and claiming the offer before we double down to that same user with enough reminder impressions to make sure they go to the store to claim their gift during the promotional window.

Interestingly, today there is still not an agreed-upon "critical mass" equation for success online, largely due to the inability to trust reported data or reluctance of advertisers and media publishers to share results publicly. With so many different KPIs, the metrics are inconclusive and rapidly changing. That being said, my hypothesis has always been to take what we know about critical mass impression share and combine it with industry acceptance of PR value. The industry standard has defined that earned value is worth 3× as much as running a paid spot because it breaks through the noise and the end user pays more attention to the content because it's being delivered to them by a trusted news anchor or via other programming. Thus, as we also know that TV/radio impressions have *more* impact on consumers than a traditional display banner ad, I concluded that in order to influence users in a digital space we should show a minimum of three times the number of display ads and extend our window of time to thirty days to provide enough time to deliver those impressions to our active audience. That then defines my remarketing goal to show *at least* twelve to twenty-one ads over seven to ten days or a minimum of thirty ads over thirty days, but just like all digital strategies, remarketing tactics must be fluid and goals change based on seasonality, industry, and the length of the sales process, which we will review in the chapters that follow.

THE CUSTOMER JOURNEY

Depending on the industry, we have different expectations of the speed that this full process will take. Typically, the larger the investment, the longer the time it takes to move the customer through the funnel. For example, if we were selling water, the most important thing at the end of the day is distribution, because if someone is thirsty, they're not going to go to another store just to find their preferred brand. It's easy to switch or influence a customer's behavior with packaging or a convenient endcap display (marketing fundamental: place). There are water brands that spend a plethora of money on ads, and yes, they can create a pattern like Fiji or Smartwater, but the bottom line is if it is not on the shelf and a prospect is thirsty, they are buying something else.

EXAMPLE PURCHASE FUNNEL: WATER	
AWARENESS	I am thirsty and need something to drink.
CONSIDERATION	What do I feel like drinking?
INTENT	Driving to the closest place to get the drink I want.
ACTION	Buying the drink and enjoying it.

Now, with a larger investment in, let's say, a solar system, we expect the customer's journey to be more thoughtful and take longer.

EXAMPLE PURCHASE FUNNEL: SOLAR	
AWARENESS	I am aware that solar exists. I have heard about it before.
CONSIDERATION	My utility bill is out of control, and I do not want to keep paying these rates. What are my other options?
INTENT	I am done with being a slave to the meter. I am going to actively start looking for a solar company near me by searching online or calling my neighbor or friend who recently got solar to learn more.
ACTION	I am requesting a free quote online or calling a solar company to schedule a solar consultation.

In some industries, like retail, it's easy to identify that a customer's journey happened because there is a solid transaction at the end. They clicked on an ad, they went to the site, they added a product to the shopping cart, and then they paid. For industries like home services, the conversion is just a lead because the sales process is longer and requires human interaction. This is very important, because when setting your online budget and planning your marketing activities calendar, we need to be able to identify all of the leads that marketing generated. What percentage of them turned into solid appointments? And from there, what percentage signed contracts? These conversion rates are critical to identify by source (paid, social, referral, organic, direct traffic) so we know how much we MUST spend online to generate the leads required to achieve our sales goals or KPIs.

When it comes to planning your company's marketing budget, there are three common ways. The first is a "percentage off the top" model, during which companies allocate a percentage of gross revenue generated over a fiscal period, that is, 3–10 percent of total earnings in 2023 will become our 2024 marketing budget. The second is the "all you can afford method," and the third and my recommended strategy is called "objective task budgeting," which means that we build a budget to support clearly identified sales goals (KPIs) and then spend what we must to generate the website traffic needed, to support each initiative: customer growth, new sales, enrollments, locations, subscribers, team members, etc.

 ANNA'S TIP

Focus on your business goals rather than on your current conversion rates to start. How many new customers do you want monthly, quarterly, annually? Of all the actual opportunities you have to present your solutions to a new qualified customer, which percentage do you win? Of all the "leads," what is your typical demo or proposal shared rate? This will serve as your new baseline to set an online budget.

In terms of KPIs, there are different types of conversion metrics online that will influence your bottom line. I like to break them out into two categories: "hard" and "soft" conversions (sometimes we call these events or goals). Hard conversions happen when a customer filled out a form, purchased something, or picked up the phone and called you, meaning you have their information and they already became a customer or are a hot sales lead, depending on your industry type. Hard conversions are worth more to your business because they indicate that you are getting closer to making money. Soft conversions are fluffier because they mean that the customer is performing actions that lead us to believe they *may* become a customer, if not on that session then on a future visit. For example, a soft conversion might be the average time someone is on your site, downloading a white paper, watching a video, or signing up for a newsletter. These actions can tell us that the user is taking steps that build consumer confidence and that they have a higher likelihood of returning on a future visit and transacting with a hard conversion.

In general, the more time someone spends on your site the higher the likelihood that they will buy something or become a customer. However, that is not always the case. They might have a long average session because they cannot find what they are looking for, which leads to high exit rates (they give up) or just really annoyed consumers. Not good for business. Hopefully, you have created an easy-to-navigate site, and the reason the customer is spending more time during that session (or visit) is because they are learning about your "leverage points of difference" or what makes you different, better, and more unique. Your website content must tell the most compelling story about your brand and engage the user to increase the speed-to-lead.

These are the first critical steps I always follow with clients. I encourage you to do this kind of thoughtful review, to see how your current website traffic is behaving and ensure that conversions are being tracked and recorded correctly.

Bottom line, just because you have a website doesn't mean that it will support your business goals for growth. It's important to be prepared to start over, even if you recently built or rebuilt your site. Your website is vital; it's where customers will meet your brand. You need to pay attention to voice, imagery, and experience.

Before we dive in, visit *thecovertcode.com* and take the quick quiz to determine your current website's score.

01000011 0110111
01101111 01100100 01100101 0010000
0010000
01101111 0110011
01101111 01100100 0110010
01101111 0110011
01101111 01100110 00100000

CHAPTER TWO

FROM AWARE TO ACTION:
YOUR CUSTOMER
AND YOUR WEBSITE

At Covert Communication, to identify a client's leverageable points of difference, we start by conducting a digital audit and brand foundations exercise. The digital audit involves a careful review of the brand's current website and social (Facebook, LinkedIn, etc.) + review sites (GoogleMyBusiness, Yelp) + listings (yellowpages, BBB) + partner profiles (solar reviews, bestcompany). The objective is to audit all our potential customers' paths or journeys online, understanding how might they find us, or what might they see, to ensure that all touch points are cohesive and contain consistent brand marks, company overview content, and contact information.

During this process, we also create some baseline expectations of what the company is selling and what their leverageable points of difference might be based on the current site design and content. Assuming they have an existing GoogleAnalytics account (and access to it), some of the useful information includes overall bounce rate, exit rates by landing page, and if conversions are tracked, the total amount by traffic source, device, and geographic region. We get an idea of existing site performance and potential opportunities.

Next, we conduct a brand foundations exercise during which we go through a series of modules with the client's identified group of key decision-makers. Depending on the size of the company and business type, this group can vary in participants from a couple of people to large groups of eight to twelve. Overall, the most important thing for a business owner to keep in mind before embarking on this process is that less is more. And they must put feelings aside. Leadership should and must set the tone for the rest of the team. Too many cooks in the kitchen can result in a less favorable outcome when it comes to branding. Personal preferences should not determine how the brand connects to its prime prospects. Once we have our group, we run through a series of three modules: Positioning Model, Brand Story, and a traditional SWOT with the additions of "aspirations" and "results." A clear vision of who we are today and the aspirations we have for tomorrow helps in building the right marketing strategy to support our "object task" budget. Our goal is to develop the right media mix that allows us to achieve sales now, while building the brand's long-term market penetration and growth.

Once we have the first series of modules completed, the agency then creates a write-up of three additional modules: Brand Brief, Brand Story, and Brand Platforms. This ensures that all team members are on the same page in their communication of the brand's value propositions to our desired target audiences. Then, with everyone on the team in agreement, the next step is to evaluate our current brand mark—the logo and tagline (if applicable)—to ensure that it is strong enough to support our brand story and will resonate with our target audiences. When evaluating a brand mark, it's critical to consider how it will be displayed online from web, tablet, and mobile devices with ranging screen sizes and resolutions. Will it look good and be readable on a super large screen in the same way as on a tiny mobile display? A logo must have both horizontal and vertical orientations; otherwise, it may be indistinguishable to a customer when viewing it cross-device as banner ads range dramatically in size and shape (square to rectangle, horizontal to vertical). Taglines are also not favorable to be used online as they become blurry, pixelated, and illegible when sized for mobile devices.

As one might imagine, asking a company to change a logo or drop a tagline that they have loved for years or even decades can be a challenge. The way that I pitch it to clients is to follow the leaders and remember that all of our favorite brands have updated their marks and continue to do so because they understand that they must to remain relevant as their audience base changes. It's no different from updating your hairstyle or replacing a sofa. It fit you then, but now it's just outdated. Styles change and many times the consumer doesn't even notice, it just feels right, familiar—it resonates. For example, did you know that Starbucks has changed their logo four times since it launched in 1971? The last update was in 2011 to commemorate their 40th anniversary with a more contemporary iteration. They're not alone. Companies like Jack-In-The-Box, Uber, and KIA, among many others, continue to update their marks to stay relevant. It doesn't mean that what we have and love is bad, it just means that it is no longer strong enough to support who we are today, or how our audience engages with our brand in a virtual space. Over the past five years, fewer than 5 percent of all Covert agency accounts have kept their original logo. From modernization of existing marks to complete rebrands, we love helping clients reimagine who they are and help them tell the most compelling story.

The next step is to create a customer journey presentation that will set the baseline for our website's site map. What content do we need to provide for each of our target audiences in order for them to move from first visit to conversion? My favorite way to organize this is by creating a matrix in which we identify what we want each unique audience to THINK, FEEL, and DO as a result of visiting our site and engaging with our content. Then, our content must SHOW, TELL, and FULFILL on the promise for each target audience to get them to convert. If the user cannot relate to the copy, images, videos, and overall sequence of consuming the content, they lose confidence and exit the site. It all matters and is especially important for companies that have multiple target audiences. Your brand must address each one uniquely and thoughtfully. Using the same content and treating all site visitors the same is one of the quickest ways to lose a sale.

The next step is to identify a click path for each target audience's customer journey so we can align on all key content required to achieve our company goals. Setting KPIs and outlining expectations are critical by audience type, as each initiative should have its own allocated budget and growth goals. Once the site goes live and we drive new paid and organic traffic to it, the user data will start to create a baseline for website traffic-to-user-conversion rates by each service offering.

Here's a real estate example of different service offerings: *sell* your home, *buy* a home, *rent* a home, *property management* for home. After enough visits, a business can make predictions whether the current media mix for each service will achieve the desired KPIs or requires a change in digital strategy.

ANNA'S TIP

Conversion rates can vary by industry based on seasonality. For retailers, Q4 is the highest grossing revenue quarter; in solar, Q3 is the hottest; for trade schools, it's Q1. You must take that into consideration when launching your solution and give your campaign enough time to work before pressing pause.

Typically, the easiest way to identify content that is not working is to view the customer page "exit" by lead source—paid or organic, that is, free traffic. If we are experiencing a high exit from the About page, then we need to review the content and adjust elements (pictures, text, headlines, structure) to see if we can change this behavior. This type of on-page optimization is one of the best ways to increase your bottom line. *Never spend* more money on generating website traffic if the traffic you are getting is not converting. I always found this concept ludicrous, and it continues to be one of the most common things I hear from business owners. Any paid traffic you generate should have some measurable result after you reach a healthy sample size. Sometimes, the answer to a problem is easy to spot and comes from a poor mobile experience, slow site load, inability for the prospective customer to navigate, or some type of bug that won't let a form be submitted, etc. It's always critical to review both mobile and desktop screen resolutions, from different devices and browsers, and to test every transaction path before launching a campaign.

Another key metric when evaluating your current website design is your bounce rate. To recap, the idea of "bounce" means that the domain visitor (user) did not make a full landing on your site before abandoning, meaning they x'd right out. The key reasons attributed to traffic bounce are: 1. It was fake traffic (bots). 2. It was human, with the most common reasons being that the website loaded too slowly, or that the content the customer saw was not what they expected to see. For example, a person searching for an electrician in California clicked on an ad and got to a website that had plumbers in California or a site for electrician equipment. Boom, they're out of there. We will cover how to ensure that doesn't happen to your business when we dive deeper into search marketing.

 ANNA'S TIP

In the new G4 Analytics, Google is now using the concept of "engaged traffic" to show how many people stayed on the site versus focusing on the number of people that didn't. So this is the metric to look at and is considered un-bounced traffic.

What is key for any business owner to understand is that you must guide and control the customer's experience as they engage with your brand online. Using drop-down menus is never a good decision because that places too much burden on the customer to pick their own path and then forces them to scroll up, and down, and up, and down. Feeling nauseous yet? This uncontrolled user experience results in the customer abandoning the visit (exiting) and moving on to the next solution to find what they're looking for, which might be your competition. Think about your own experiences online. The sites that you've bought from or continue to visit have created a journey that is easy and enjoyable. You can find what you are looking for fast (people skim first and then read) and they provide ways for you to engage and dive deeper when applicable.

ANNA'S TIP

Never use drop-down menus on your website. It places the burden on the customer to pick a path. You want to guide them on their journey. Organize content using internal menus, tabs, or toggles to make sure customers don't get lost or confused on their way to conversion.

Engagement for the modern consumer means toggles, tabs, recommendations, infographics, video content, chat, or applications like calculators, quizzes, or games. Consumers want choices but are still driven by the need to be led. There is also a concept of "fatigue" when the customer has too many choices and, out of fear that they will make the wrong one, makes none. This was first proven in a jam study in 2000 by psychologist Sheena Iyengar and Mark Lepper.[3] During the study, they offered either twenty-four jam options or six. Sales increased when the customer had only six selections to choose from. Since then, advertisers have learned that three, not six, is the magic number in terms of increasing purchase. The reason? With three choices, the consumer can easily remove one option out of consideration, leaving themselves with two. Then they pick a winner, and feel in control and happy with their decision. Any more than three recommended options and the brain starts to question what you truly want, resulting in you buying nothing out of fear of making the wrong choice.

We see this a lot in the solar industry when customers get too many competitor proposals. They panic because so much is on the line in terms of investment, and they have so little knowledge about what they are actually purchasing. With so many variables and high stakes,

---

3   Sheena S. Iyengar and Mark R. Lepper, "When Choice Is Demotivating: Can One Desire Too Much of a Good Thing?" *Journal of Personality and Social Psychology* 79, no. 6 (2000), https://faculty.washington.edu/jdb/345/345%20Articles/Iyengar%20&%20Lepper%20(2000).pdf.

they freeze up and are not able to trust that they will pick the right partner, products, or financing, and drop out of the market. They may be unhappy with their rising utility bill, but at least they know how it works and what to expect. The modern consumer is all about me, me, me. Finding the right fit means that you are reaching them in the way they want, with messaging they care about. That journey starts online and translates all the way through the sales process, taking the shape of drip emails, text automations, and scripting once a customer has completed a conversion on your site, such as a sale, in-bound call, or lead form completed. A break in the tone of voice, imagery, or messaging confuses customers, causing them to doubt or not trust your company. And once trust is lost, it's hard to get back.

Our job is to help the customer find what they are looking for, and then, hopefully, not regret their decision later. I always thought it was laughable that agencies and media partners care so much about the client's product and will quickly blame them for customer burn but never hold themselves to the same standards. They overpromise and underdeliver on their goods, and the result is the same: unhappy clients that leave. Part of this stems from a lack of communication and setting the right expectations on what their product will yield. Even companies providing great products and services can find themselves on the chopping block for not educating the client or asking the right questions. You might be doing exactly what is in your SOW (scope of work) or product description, but if the client does not speak the same lingo, or misinterprets your solutions, you're toast. It's critical to remain transparent and set clear expectations for how your products or services will help the client/customer solve their problem.

Now that we are on the same page as to the process, let's go through an agency case study of how to identify the client's leverage points of difference, create a customer journey, design a click path, and execute a win online!

Remember that a company's website designs change all the time, much more frequently than brand marks, and for good reason. Customers' online shopping behavior is evolving, and unless your brand stays relevant in design and features, it's not going to generate results. The good news for business owners is that your website is not a printed brochure (expensive) and can change fast. If built on platforms like WordPress, it is easy to update without code (cheap). Think about your website design just like any part of your brand identity. It's a living entity and, as your business changes, so should your site. I always share with my clients to not get caught up in details like a featured picture or a paragraph of copy. Launch the site, let the hard work start, and then we can fuss about design.

 ANNA'S TIP

Print out the brand foundations exercise annually and then review your responses year-over-year. See what is different (if anything) about your team's answers and then review your current website's content. Yes, reread everything. Ask yourself if your brand's direction is still aligned with your current site's copy, imagery, and site map.

CASE STUDY: MIRASOL SOLAR

I was first introduced to Mirasol FAFCO Solar, located in Sarasota, Florida, in December 2020, during the COVID-19 pandemic. The client had been interviewing agencies and, although at first they were reluctant to work with a Hawaii-based company, Zoom was redefining the way businesses engaged and normalized the concept of working remotely. After a few meetings, they saw the value of our deep solar experience and existing partnership with SunPower and took the leap. Since then, they have experienced a 4× growth in sales and recently launched a complementary solar company, Manatee Solar, servicing Jacksonville residents, and have added EV charging to their service offerings. The agency started with our brand foundations exercise and learned that Mirasol was a family-owned and operated local installer with 40+ years' experience in the marketplace. As early adopters, they were established with a strong background in solar pool and water heating and had expanded to traditional photovoltaic (PV) solar focusing on both residential and commercial customers. From our exercise, we learned that they were seen as a local, trusted leader and were deeply committed to the community. Another key leverageable point of difference was that, unlike most solar companies, Mirasol would provide service and maintenance to residents whose installation was from another company. This is a big deal, because there are over one million orphaned solar homeowners in America today. That means that either the solar manufacturer, the solar sales company, or the solar installer are no longer in business (or in some cases all three may be unreachable). Most solar contractors reject maintenance jobs on systems not installed by their team because of roof penetration risks or other concerns about a poor installation that they may inherit. As the saying goes, "the last man on the roof" is the one who becomes responsible—not a burden many business owners want to undertake. But Mirasol viewed this as a service to the community (especially with the growing number of hurricanes) and had built a profitable service department providing panel cleanings, system checks, removal, and repair, earning them a strong reputation and favorable residual revenue.

During the initial digital audit and brand foundations exercise, it became clear that the client's existing brand mark and website design did not align with their brand story or growth goals. Although pool heating had been their bread and butter, times were changing, and they wanted to focus efforts on traditional PV. The client's logo and brand mark also contained "FAFCO," which is the name of the leader in solar  pool heating manufacturing and had been incorporated to ensure that customers quickly associated them with the best products available. The agency recommended removing FAFCO and reinventing the logo to include the full sun, which was more memorable, easier to identify in icon sizes, and aligned with their approach. There was nothing "half" about this brand! During the logo discovery, we presented three updated versions and they picked the second one.

Then we moved to the customer journey presentation, which helps us identify our site map and expected click paths. The agency identified that the core target audiences were residential homeowners, business owners, developers, and news/media. We outlined those in our THINK, FEEL, and DO matrix and provided a recommended new site map that will allow us to create content to develop SHOW, TELL, and FULFILL for our customer objectives.

MIRASOL MATRIX

ACTION	HOMEOWNERS	BUSINESS OWNERS	DEVELOPERS	NEWS & MEDIA
THINK	Mirasol is highly qualified and local. I believe that they really want to help me save with solar.	Mirasol can get the job faster and more efficiently than others in the market. They have a good reputation.	Mirasol is safer than other companies because they have the best product, team, and knowledge.	Mirasol is really setting a new standard for solar businesses in Florida.
FEEL	I feel relieved and grateful that Mirasol cares more about helping me go solar than they care about money.	I feel assured that my project will be in the best hands, will not go over budget, and will be installed by the most qualified team. I trust them.	I feel optimistic about the future and know that with Mirasol my upcoming projects will be completed on time and budget.	I'm amazed the company has come so far so fast, and excited to see what they're going to do next.
DO	I'm going to visit the website, use the solar wizard, call, or stop by the showroom and get started.	I'm going to visit the website, use solar wizard, set up a meeting and get a good deal on my project, and then refer Mirasol to my friends.	I'm going to set up a meeting and include Mirasol on all my bids and plans moving forward.	I'm going to sign up for their newsletter to keep tabs on what's going on.

Our content design must show, tell, and fulfill the promise. Essentially, this means that we must demonstrate our expertise with featured projects, customer reviews, industry awards, product or team videos, and other types of content that explain our story and leverageable points of difference. Functionable feature sets should also be considered, such as a live chat, calculator plug-in, events calendar, forum, blog, ability to leave a review, etc., to help create more value and establish a deeper connection with our audiences.

From our exercise, we identified problems with the existing navigation. The site had drop-downs and was organized by service offering rather than audience type: About Us | Solar Electric PV Systems | Water Heating | Pool Heating | Pool Controls | Cool PV | Gallery | Contact. This left website visitors with too many options to consider, as it was unclear which solution was right for them. They had little knowledge about the difference in these technologies and had no way to quickly dive into the core content that mattered, that is, I want to save money on my electric bill, but how?

The client's recommended site map became this: Logo (home) | About | Residential | Commercial | Projects | Reviews | Solar Calculator | Service Requests | News | Free Quote and then we supported that with secondary and in some instances tertiary sub-navigation pages of content. This allows the customer to quickly navigate to the right content and controls their experience versus traditional drop-downs.

There are several options to accomplish this structurally online, including a secondary menu right beneath the menu bar, as on Mirasol's site, or design vertically down the side panel of a website. Tabs or toggles can be used within the page to quickly help customers find what they are looking for without requiring them to visit a new page, which is ideal (super-fast shopping).

Let's take this opportunity to do a quick audit of your site. Can customers quickly navigate without the need to visit a new page or scroll up/down? What about in mobile? If the customer is looking for something specific, do you allow for a search? If so, try searching for something you think should be easy to find on our site and see what the results are.

Next, we walk through a series of customer journey examples to identify motivational triggers and potential click paths that the audiences may take. This way, once we start to drive traffic to the website, we will be able to quickly identify any bottlenecks in content or exit rates before conversion.

Most company websites have the same motivational triggers: Learn, Buy, Help, or Engage. Customer journeys start off the page (somewhere) and then end on the page (your domain), meaning that the customer has the opportunity to encounter your brand in various ways before ending up at your URL. This concept is directly aligned with the purchase funnel and will be critical as you build your media budget to achieve desired KPIs.

 ANNA'S TIP

Trust your instincts and keep it simple. Overthinking this journey is a waste of your time. The most important thing is that you understand the concept that different users will come to your site for unique reasons, and we must show them what is most important for them.

Let's review a customer journey example and click paths as we identified them using the Mirasol example. It's important to mention that although we know that customers may enter our site from other landing pages, not just the home page, we always start our journey with the home page as the initial click because we will be able to control the customer's journey from paid advertising, which is more important to business owners as it directly impacts their bottom line.

Example Customer Journey Learn:
Jim and his wife are retired snowbirds and spend the summers in Colorado and the rest of the year in Florida. Jim is in bed scrolling through pictures of his grandkids on Facebook when he sees a video about "going solar" and how he can replace his ever-growing utility bill with a fixed payment to ease his retirement. He clicks on the ad to learn more about the Mirasol Solar Difference.

Starting on "Home" the customer may then pick these paths:

- Path 1—About > Services > Residential > Incentives > Financing
- Path 2—Residential > Technology > Warranty > Reviews
- Path 3—Reviews > Projects > Residential > Solar Calculator > About
- CTAs along the way -> Try Solar Calculator, Submit Free Quote, Start Live Chat, Schedule a Consultation or subscribe to email newsletter.

To wrap up the presentation, we identify the types of content that our website will contain, which includes text, images, video, and applications. We clearly outline what pixels and plug-ins will be installed on the site, and then outline a launch timeline.

Once we have final approval, the agency either custom designs a website starting in photoshop/illustrator or uses an existing template and customizes it for the client. After the site is launched, the real fun begins with submission of the sitemap to Google Search Console, launch of digital ad campaign, and a press release to boost off-site SEO (all topics that we will cover in upcoming chapters!).

Website Reimagined

BEFORE

AFTER

Lastly, even as I recap this case study, I'm reminded of how important it is to continue to review your company's service offerings annually. As your company grows and matures, each new initiative must be designed and deployed with clear KPIs, tracking, and budgets in mind. Many of you might be feeling overwhelmed, and that's OK. The next chapter will help identify the various frameworks and content management systems (CMSs) available on which to build your website and why those choices directly impact your online results. This includes not only where your website is hosted, but what website builder you choose and how to hire the right company to build one for you.

01000011 0110111
01101111 01100100 01100101 0010000
0010000
01101111 0110011
01101111 01100100 0110010
01101111 0110011
01101111 01100110 00100000

CHAPTER THREE

MAKING THE RIGHT TECHNOLOGY CHOICES

For business owners, everything comes down to choice. From building your team to picking your technology stack, what separates those who thrive from those who fail is understanding how to navigate all those daily choices to achieve your short-term and long-term business goals. While consumer buying behavior changes relatively slowly, technology is rapidly accelerating. The website framework or customer relationship management (CRM) system your team used in the past with success might now be impacting your company's ability to stay competitive and thrive. Being able to know when to pivot and how to assess your tech stack is imperative to staying relevant and continuing to meet and exceed both team and customer expectations.

I'm often asked how I acquired the knowledge that has moved my business into a position of authority as a digital expert, and it all boiled down to one key choice that I made in 2010 to learn WordPress.

At the time, it was out of necessity. I had herniated L4 and L5 in my back and was undergoing physical therapy when the owner of Harris Therapy asked me if I could build her a website and help her with some online ads. My first instinct was to say "no," but an old boyfriend of mine had recently shared that he had started installing WordPress websites to increase revenue for his photography business. I was surprised because he couldn't write a line of code. I felt confident that if he could do it, so could I.

Thus, my online journey began. I went home that night and called him for some tips, which included filtering by the best sellers or most popular template themes, which helped guarantee that there was clear documentation and support should I run into any problems. Then, assuming the client's domain was hosted on GoDaddy, they had a quick setup for the WordPress environment. After that, all you had to do was follow the documentation. I did just that and launched harristherapy.com five weeks later. Then I built another site and another and another. It was not always easy, and I made plenty of mistakes, like the time that I deleted Hospice Hawaii's mySQL database while trying to install a new template, but it became a pivotal tool in my career.

Today, I install on average one site a week and won't even agree to help a client with digital marketing unless I am in complete control of the user's experience. It just does not work. If they think their site is good enough, or their logo and content are compelling, then the door swings that way. As a female business owner, it's sometimes difficult to put your foot down. I remember a client scolding me after a meeting with his boss: "The client is always right and you need to give him what he wants." But the fact is that they are not "always" right. Something isn't working—that's why they hired me.

I've learned to be blunt when necessary—like right now. It's not about you. It's about your customer. One of the most important actions you can take is to take a comprehensive look at your user's experience from their perspective, not yours.

I'll never forget when I was marketing director for Paul Brown Salons & Spas (my first job out of college) and we were launching the Paul Brown Institute of Beauty & Wellness Technologies. The launch included a full media plan with TV, radio, print, and social media. Since we had a limited budget, I elected to run ads on selective stations, such as sponsoring *Shear Genius* and *America's Next Top Model*. Then, the owner said, "I want to see my ads on the news." I explained to him that our audience was not watching the news and asked how much was it worth to him to see his spot air. Was he planning to attend beauty school? If not, why was he assuming that his perspective was the same as his customer?

The same goes for overall design and taste. That's why, when electing to work with an advertising agency or hiring a designer, it's important to ask for samples of their work to make sure you agree on the fundamental aesthetics of design. If it's a match and you like other work they have produced, then you can rest assured that you will be happy with the final results, as long as you follow their lead.

WEBSITE FRAMEWORKS

Web development frameworks are also referred to as web application frameworks or simply web frameworks. They're a collection of tools and resources that help developers build and manage applications like a website. Frameworks come in many shapes and sizes. What is most important for a business owner is to pick a solution that you are in control of, meaning that you will not require a developer to make content, image, or product changes. Yes, there will always be the need for developers, but unless you're part of a really large corporation or dealing with data that has security risks (i.e., banks, healthcare, or insurance), the cost-effective and best choice is to pick a CMS that will allow anyone on the team to easily make changes without requiring coding. When picking your CMS, I recommend two distinct paths based on the industry type: retail versus non-retail.

 ANNA'S TIP

Before you pick a framework, identify all the user experiences from your customer journey exercise. Will you need an events calendar? Does your site need to take a payment? Will you be storing personal information? Will your site be multilingual? These features and functions must be available via website plug-ins for any framework you choose to ensure you keep your development costs low and installation time fast.

RETAIL SOLUTIONS

For retailers who will be transactional online and require a shopping cart, the best solutions are Shopify and BigCommerce. Shopify is the clear winner unless you require a wholesale login and unique pricing, in which case BigCommerce is the better choice as they include this in their feature pricing suite while Shopify charges a fee (which I feel is really unfair, as it doesn't cost them anything additional to allow customers to access this feature set). That being said, if you do not require a wholesale login or have a large enough network to warrant the additional monthly cost, Shopify is the superior choice as they offer an easy-to-use backend and a plethora of beautiful templates, integrations, and plug-ins.

NON-RETAIL SOLUTIONS

For non-retail sites, there are several popular CMS solutions, including WordPress, Drupal, Joomla, Moodel, Webflow, MODX, and Weebly. As I'm sure you know by now, my recommendation is to use WordPress. You can also go to themeforest.net and purchase a wide variety of excellent themes; my personal favorite is Avada. In fact, since 2016, the agency hasn't installed anything on another theme, and on those few occasions when we do have to work on a site not installed by the agency, we have a full team Slack channel filled with complaints when having to update a client's design editor on elementor or divi, which requires a lot of learning when compared with the intuitive and complete solution provided by Avada.

When developing a site, you have two options: you can either use an existing template or you can custom-design a site in photoshop/ illustrator and then have a developer code it into a custom template on the desired framework (WordPress/Shopify). At Covert Communication, we do both. For 90 percent of clients, we will pick an Avada theme and then customize it. For the other 10 percent who want something breakout, we design a site first and then code it into Avada for long-term accessibility and easy-to-build pages/add plug-ins. This can be low cost if you work with the right developer who will just create the basic elements of the custom theme and then, once you have those created, anyone can build all the rest of the pages in the approved sitemap without a line of code (like me!).

ANNA'S TIP

Always look at the total number of active installations before picking a theme. Avada has over 900K active installations with 25K 5-star ratings. This guarantees that they will always support the product and continue to invest in new features and designs. Don't pick a partner that hasn't updated to the latest version of WordPress and has fewer than 40K installations.

WHAT ARE PLUG-INS?

Plug-ins are components that you can add to your website design to speed up the installation. Before CRMs came into existence, websites were hard coded into HTML and each function had to be developed from scratch—everything from form submissions to video sliders. Plug-ins allow a company to pick from thousands of features for free or with a low monthly subscription for pro elements that instantly add features to a site with no code required. For example, my plug-in Trusting Solar Calculator, a.k.a. Solar Wizard, offers solar companies an easy-to-use solar calculator that homeowners and business owners can use during their research phase to help answer questions like: "How much solar do I need?" "How much will I save?" "What will it cost?" for a low monthly subscription. Instead of a solar company having to commission a developer to create a calculator from scratch, they can simply subscribe and immediately provide customers with this enhanced experience to lift conversion rates. When a customer's questions are answered, they feel more confident in supplying their contact information and moving on to the next phase in the process: receiving their no-obligation custom quote.

SHOPIFY/RETAIL COMMON PLUG-INS

- loyalty programs
- promo banners that feature offers like free shipping
- pop-ups like subscribe with a discount on first order
- find a retailer near you search function
- currency converters
- spin the wheel and win games

COMMON WORDPRESS PLUG-INS

- Form builders like ContactForm7 (free) or Formidable Forms (paid but includes ways to securely upload and store documents)
- YOAST, which is a plug-in to help with your site SEO
- LayerSlider
- Reorder Posts (to reorganize posts or portfolio items)
- Events Calendar
- WooCommerce, which is a shopping plug-in/platform that works on WordPress. My recommendation is to only use WooCommerce if you are selling something digital in nature, like a book download or very limited product SKUs.

SHOPIFY TEMPLATES

When choosing a Shopify template, the features and functionality you may want to look for include the ability to "quick shop," which means the customer is not redirected to the shopping cart after adding a product. You also want the option for variable products based on size/color for each style. Many older templates do not allow for this, which means that you would have to add a unique product into the catalog for each color, even if the product is the same. Other new templates offer built-in features, such as promotional banners and pop-ups, to opt into an email/text campaign. Another key reason to pick Shopify is its partnership with Yotpo and SMS Boost, which allows easy-to-use texting capabilities, loyalty program, and automated reviews collection (and customer rewards!). So now, instead of sending emails to all customers through a mail program like MailChimp, you can curate a targeted list of shoppers and text them based on their purchase history to increase conversions. Did you know that 98 percent of text messages are opened, while it is believed that only 20 percent of emails are opened?[4] The result is a higher conversion rate and more targeted campaigns. For example, let's say I purchased a Paradise Aloha Shirt from Hilo Hattie in blue and left a 4-star review on my purchase. Flash forward a few months. Now they've added the same shirt in red. SMS boost would allow Hilo Hattie to send me a text message announcing this new arrival and motivate me to purchase without a discount: Your Favorite Shirt Is Back! Limited Availability, Grab Yours Before They're Gone.

Taking a slight deviation from frameworks, let's talk more about recurring weekly online sales promotions for retailers, as this can make or break your business. Conceptually, I believe it's a mistake for

---

4   "Email marketing statistics, 2023" and "Texting statistics, 2023" Truelist, 2023, https://truelist. co/blog/email-marketing-statistics/; https://truelist.co/blog/texting-statistics/.

retailers to create patterns that train customers to wait for discounts, essentially devaluing the brand. Of course, all retailers must have those big holiday sales, or they lose out to competitors, but committing to weekly recurring sales creates negative behavior by training the customer to very regularly expect a discount. This results in reduced margins and, in the long term, can put companies at serious financial risk. One classic example I learned about at Bentley University was shared in a Harvard Business School study titled "Coca-Cola vs. Pepsi-Cola and the Soft Drink Industry,"[5] which describes the competition dilemma created by the two companies. Essentially, every other week one brand would go on sale, thus training the customer to wait to buy soda (or to buy the competitor's product) and so dropping the margin per can for both brands.

Moreover, it's important for brands to understand that promotions don't work forever. There is a mathematical equation that shows the exact unit at which a company will make a profit and then every unit sold after that results in a loss of revenue. The reason for this is usually related to inventory supply, because manufacturing new products takes time, and the chances are the cost of the goods or some fee along the manufacturing or sales channel will not be the same as it was when the last batch was acquired. For example, if you had two million units of chips and knew that if you sold them for $1.20 a bag you would make a 50¢ profit on each, the next batch of chips you order might require you to sell them for $2 per bag to make the same profit. But now there are coupons in the market with double-sales days or a percentage off. Cash flow is going down fast.

Another easy-to-recognize scam that many readers may have been bamboozled by is Groupon. Yes, it's fast money and instant visibil-

---

5   Michael E. Porter, "Coca-Cola vs. Pepsi-Cola and the soft drink industry," Harvard Business School, March 1991, https://www.hbs.edu/faculty/Pages/item.aspx?num=12066.

ity, but to continue offering services at less than 50 percent doesn't result in growing a customer base because those coupon clippers will *never* pay full price. So now you have alienated your actual target audience (existing customers) by booking up and limiting appointments to accommodate this surge of new business. But once all the coupons are used, the phone calls dry up. The unfortunate result? The business owner is in such a panic to make payroll and manage cash flow that they do it all over again. These discounts have put many small companies out of business.

 ANNA'S TIP

Try to plan out your promotions at the beginning of the year centered around holidays and do the math before creating online sales. Create best-case and worst-case scenarios and then only if you MUST generate cash flow quickly should you break from the plan. Create other opportunities to increase sales from your existing customer base using targeted messaging and more urgency with limited product releases or presales— no promo required.

WHEN TO MIX AND MATCH FRAMEWORKS

There are times when it's a good decision to mix and match frameworks. The agency has done this several times to get the best of both worlds for clients who have unique business verticals (service offerings). For example, DiamondBakery.com, one of Hawaii's most famous Made-in-Hawaii brands, recently added fundraising to their product mix. The agency identified that their custom Shopify website did not contain enough functionality to provide the best user experience to support that audience because of limited page-builder elements and ways to showcase text/video content or allow for the required secure form submission with custom fields. For that reason, we recommended moving any content *unrelated* to "shop" into a WordPress template with a matching design. For the customer, it is a seamless experience; they do not know that they are leaving the shopping site. The only way for laypeople to tell is to look at the domain. If you click on About or Fundraising (any page outside of the shop), you will see the domain swap to about.diamondbakery. com, referred to as a subdomain. This is where we installed a WordPress Avada theme with custom design.

DOMAIN REGISTRATIONS AND HOSTING

Once you determine your website framework, you will need to consider domain registration and website hosting. I can't stress enough the importance that you *never ever* should let another company or individual at your organization register a domain name for you. When registering your domain name, *always* use a .com ending as any other type of domain will reduce your ability to reach the desired audience and will increase the cost of your paid media campaigns. That being said, it is also recommended to purchase close alternates of your desired registered domain for brand protection. This means that, if you want to register company.com, you should also purchase companies.com, company.net, company.info, thecompany.com, etc.

Once you have your domain registered, the next topic is where to host your website. As a best practice, I never recommend hosting your domain and website with the same company. Why? Because if something goes wrong, you're toast. Maybe the company goes out of business; maybe someone is in a car accident; maybe you are in a payment dispute; whatever may happen, it's just too risky. I have experienced countless things going wrong and hearts broken when domains are lost forever or cost thousands to reactivate.

 ANNA'S TIP

Always maintain ownership of your domain and never give anyone your login. If someone requires access, you can grant them "delegate" access to your account using their email, protecting your property.

I personally register domains on GoDaddy.com, but refer to them for all other services as a strong "NoDaddy" from so many negative experiences. I'll never forget in 2015 when I was introduced to Makana Esthetics Wellness Academy. In our second meeting, I had proposed a new website installation for the client before starting any paid ads. The founder, Malia Sanchez, was walking me through how they knew they needed a new site but wanted to start with fixing the old site. When we pulled up their site, it went to a strange error page—not the typical 404 page. What we saw were search results for a refrigeration company. Malia's husband Jeff jumped on the phone with GoDaddy and, after forty-five minutes, it was determined that someone had hacked their site and no, GoDaddy did not have any backups. The hacker had gone into the archive as well, and there was nothing that could be done. Malia then turned to me and asked, "This isn't some marketing scheme to build us a new website, is it?" I assured them that I would have something up quickly and, over the weekend, installed a site that not only met but exceeded all expectations. The client was thrilled, but that was the first strike against the giant. Then, over the next two years, several more hacks occurred and I had just about enough. Also, I think it's highly unethical to charge clients for services not rendered. Make sure with any service provider that you have an option to leave with a refund if you're not satisfied with the services you receive. For example, if you purchase a website hosting package for two years and then want to leave after one year, make sure they will issue a refund and you won't be locked in to a promotional rate. It's just another way for them to take advantage of business owners who paid early. It should be prorated, you pay for what you use, not what you don't use. That's fair.

My favorite hosting is with WPengine.com, which offers premium support, SSL certificates, and up to three environments (production or live site, staging, and development copies of your site for added layers of security and testing), all under a single plan with a very competitive monthly/annual cost. It's the fastest and most secure WordPress hosting available. They have even detected that one of our client's IP was being hacked and, without seeking approval, dynamically changed it in the backend to prevent the hack. This is not a service offered by others, and in fact could have resulted in a massive loss in revenue and long-term damage to a brand. Think of Russian hackers stealing your site and putting up a clock with demands to pay by a specific date or it will be deleted.

Other superior hosting providers include digitalocean.com and of course AWS.com or Amazon Web Services, which is the most sophisticated and comprehensive one around. One thing to mention is that if you pick Shopify or BigCommerce as your retail framework, they *are* the hosting company as well as the framework. So, you just need to point your domain and you'll be killing two birds with one stone. That's why they charge a monthly fee. It includes both the framework and hosting of the site. WordPress is open source and free to use, but does not include a hosting solution.

WHAT IS OPEN SOURCE?

Open source means that the developer code used to write the solution is open and anyone can inspect, modify, and enhance it. A good example of this relates to application development for Android (GooglePlay) versus Apple (IOS). When creating a plug-in on Android, you can publish the application without any approval because it's open source. If you want to publish that same application on the Apple Developer Store, it must go through approval as AppleIOS is closed source. Some of the most common examples of open-source software include WordPress, Drupal, Firefox, Java Script, Python, and Parse. The benefits of open-source technologies are that they provide a platform to continue to learn from others and enhance the features. Open source is a very cost-effective investment for companies because it prevents what's known as "vendor lock-in," which can result in higher costs to maintain software as well as adding flexibility to modify and enhance it by anyone with code skills. Closed source is considered proprietary software like Microsoft— companies are bound by the defined terms and conditions that are provided by the license, so no one can make Excel or PowerPoint do something special that is not already a feature set. Make sense?

 ANNA'S TIP

Always pick an open-source software to keep costs low and ensure you have the control and choice to use another developer or partner at any time.

Now that we have picked an easy-to-use framework and have control over our domain and hosting, it's time to pick a CRM tool, which will manage all company leads and report the source—paid ads, customer referrals, events, etc. Picking the right tool is critical; otherwise, you will not be able to determine if the money you are spending on your marketing is achieving your business goals. Our mission is to be able to track conversions by marketing initiative and drill down to the cost-per-lead, cost-per-appointment, and cost-per-sale generated.

HOW TO CHOOSE YOUR TECH STACK TO SCALE

Did you know that today most enterprise organizations subscribe to nearly a hundred types of software? Many of these programs are not used at all, or are only being used by a segment of the team to their full potential. The result? Thousands of dollars lost in recurring fees. Reviewing your organization's tech stack and removing redundancies is one of the easiest ways to increase revenue while speeding up production. At Covert, we call this a company's technology transformation. It all starts with a list of demands. What do we want our customers' experience to be and how will we fulfill that using the technology at our disposal? This experience must be transcendent because, although painful for many companies, it is the only way to operate in an evolving digital landscape. Thinking about your company size today and what it will become tomorrow matters, especially when considering which CRMs are best to manage leads and projects. There are many types of CRMs, but the most common are Salesforce, Zoho, Pipedrive, HubSpot, JobNimbus, GoHighLevel (GHL), and Netsuite.

The biggest problem with CRMs has always been the pricing models. There are three common ways to be billed: by user count, by features, or by the number of contacts in your database. In some instances, like with HubSpot, they may bill you all three ways for your active subscription. In fact, for most companies, I have found that less than 5 percent of the seated team members require access to pro features like premium reporting. Even so, every user is still required to be on the same monthly subscription. I refer to this as "gating" and find it incredibly unethical as it costs the software company nothing to open up features to all users and to determine ways to charge based on usage. These common pricing models make CRMs one of the most expensive operating costs for medium to large business owners and unaffordable for small business owners. With an average cost of $100 per user, even to support a small team of five becomes $500 a month and $6,000 annual commitment. While that doesn't sound like a lot of money, compared to using Excel or GoogleSheets for free it adds up, especially when not being utilized to the fullest potential. Beyond price per user, the ability to scale up and down your feature set is also key. For example, if you were in the retail business, you'd want to be able to send out more drip email campaigns or text message offers over Q4 than in Q1, right? Depending on the CRM you choose, you might have to increase your subscription to accommodate those emails in-season and be unable to decrease the plan off-season.

Next, we get to the concept of charging by database contacts. It's important to note that there were new rules put forth by the California Privacy Rights Act (CPRA) in 2023 that were implemented several years ago in the European Union. They outline General Data Protection Regulations and provide guidelines on how long a company can retain customer data and how they can acquire it. Depending on your industry and business size, it's recommended to consult a lawyer to make sure that your company is fully compliant and has protocols in place to purge old data, as well as ways for consumers to opt out. For smaller/medium organizations, there are sites like Osana.com that provide legal guidance, easy-to-use products, and support to ensure that you are protected.

 ANNA'S TIP

A great partner in this space is Osana.com, which offers a pixel and backend to manage all things related to ensuring your business is meeting global obligations online with cookie preferences, and secure forms to request account deletion, etc. They also are so confident that their worldwide solutions are top-notch that if a protected domain is the subject of a lawsuit, they will cover $200K worth of legal fees. Great support and highly recommended!

Now back to paying per contact. With this new knowledge on how long you can hold a contact, it's important to maintain a scrubbed database and protect the integrity of your brand by practicing universal opt-out. This means that if someone says "take me off your list" at your call center, you immediately remove that customer from text and email campaigns. Yes, this should include Facebook and other types of direct messaging via social if you are implementing those strategies in your marketing outreach efforts. This might seem like a lot of work but there are CRM solutions that offer these features (either included or for a paid upgrade) and far less effort than a lawsuit! Companies must have clear communication expectations outlined on how they will work leads and then continue to engage with customers in the future. This boils down to a key concept: How did we get the leads data and did they opt in? It's very common for businesses to get into trouble when acquiring lists from partners or buying aged data from a provider.

When purchasing lists, always make sure that your provider includes a TrustedForm certification, meaning that they have proof that the customer did opt in to be contacted (they have a recording of this IP submitting a form and take responsibility for the lead in the event of a lawsuit). There are also important things to consider even if you did acquire verified opt-in third-party data. For example, if you wanted to send an email campaign to those users through MailChimp or Constant Contact, you could be putting your domain in jeopardy of being flagged as spam. The reason for this is that those emails you purchased did not opt in to receive emails from *your* domain and most likely do not know who you are. This results in a high spam rate, meaning that the customers who received the email marked your message as spam. If this number is higher than 0.1 percent, it will indicate to your mailing provider that your list is of poor quality. That then places a hold on your mailing program account, which impacts your company's ability to send messages to actual customers who did opt in. It can also have long-lasting negative results by permanently damaging your domain, that is, when someone from your team sends an email, it goes directly to the customer's junk folder. Once a domain is marked as malicious, it's nearly impossible to have that flag removed. In this case, the only option a company would have is to change their email domain, which is disruptive to the team and results in missed opportunities and brand confusion. I always recommend that if you "make a deal" with a partner to share lists or cross-promote services, the email should come from that company to their customers introducing the partner with a clear opt in. For example, if Diamond Bakery and Hilo Hattie wanted to cross-promote Made-in-Hawaii products, Hilo Hattie would send an email to its subscribers sharing Diamond Bakery as a partner with a special coupon code offer and link to "opt in" to Diamond Bakery's list link. Then the same email would be sent out from Diamond Bakery promoting Hilo Hattie.

 ANNA'S TIP

Don't ever upload a list from a third party into your email program without first running a verified double-opt-in message. This can also be accomplished from your mail provider, but ask yourself, is it worth it? With so much noise and email clutter, what do you think the likelihood of someone opening your email is without any previous interaction with your brand? If they did open it, will they be happy that you found them or annoyed? Don't put your brand in the junk category. This type of strategy is a dead end.

The same rules apply for business texting. Effective summer of 2023, a new requirement was introduced called A2P 10DLC, which stands for Application-to-Person messaging using a 10-Digit Long Code phone number. This new requirement mandates that any text message sent from a technology application be considered "business texting" and must be registered, even if it is person-to-person. This process was set forth by carriers to reduce spam/fraud and the good news is that, once registered, it increases your company's text delivery rate by providing a layer of confidence that your messages will not be flagged or blocked. This is a legal requirement and companies can be subject to penalties if they do not comply. In order to register a company number, business owners will be required to submit an EIN as well as answer questions regarding which types of text campaigns you will be engaging in and proof that you are allowing customers to opt in and opt out of messaging.

There are several different types of technology applications that companies can use to deliver text messages to customers, but my recommendation is to include this knowledge into your CRM wish list, as the fewer tools in your tech stack the more effective you will be. We've all heard the expression "too many cooks in the kitchen" and this sentiment resonates exceptionally well with technology. The result, your customer got a really bland steak and is not coming back to your restaurant (who was responsible for the salt again?). The same is true with communications; if your team has to login to a specific app to retrieve customer texts and another for emails, things get missed and that results in a potential lead having a negative experience. Let's dive deeper.

Just like picking a website framework and outlining your website's plug-in requirements, the first step to picking the right CRM for your business is conducting a discovery with your team and outlining process requirements by department to create a features wish list. Here's a list of questions to get you started:

- How many people on your team touch a lead?
- How many ways does your company get a lead, that is, number of sources? Do you treat those efforts differently and how?
- How do you book appointments currently?
- Are you using Outlook or Gmail as your primary email? (this matters when it comes to technology, since Gmail plays nicely with others (one click login), Microsoft typically does not).
- What is the average time it takes to move a customer from lead to sale?
- How are you currently engaging with customers post-lead? Email, text, phone calls?
- How many times do you reach out to a customer during the sales process, and in which ways? x calls per day, x texts per week, x emails per month, etc.

- Are you recording calls and tracking numbers? In-bound and out-bound?
- Are you engaging in social media? If so, which channels and how often do you post?
- Are you asking for reviews from customers? How often?
- Do you send surveys to your customers?
- Do you require billing integrations?
- Do you generate a proposal from a third party? What is required to call a job closed by sales (signed contract, copy of intake form, uploaded documents, etc.)?

Now do the same thing with your operations team, identifying the tools they need to be successful to manage a customer post-sale. This might include a scheduling tool to dispatch a crew, creating a PO, ordering equipment, printing a packing slip, or pulling a permit.

Feel like a lot of work? It can be, depending on your company's size, but for most small/medium organizations it's fairly straightforward. Over the past few years, my agency has become known for solving complex technology problems and helping companies streamline processes from lead indigestion (that means creation of the lead in the CRM) all the way to fulfillment (contract sold or project complete). With leads becoming increasingly expensive, companies simply cannot afford to lose any opportunity. It is critical that leadership have control over data messaging, communications strategies, and a way to evaluate the success of marketing efforts by source, from lead all the way to sale and beyond (we will dive deeper into this in chapter 4 on what a customer is worth).

So, let's unpack the concept of what we call "Speed-to-Lead" and how to pick the right CRM solution to create the best opportunity to win. I like to break CRM decisions into two main categories: sales focused and operations focused. Just like we do for website frameworks, organizations can mix and match CRMs, and we often do this with our clients to get the best of both worlds (enhanced features at a lower cost). But that should only be considered with the help of a technology consultant (like us), as it requires custom code and is not something that should be rushed into without careful planning. For example, we often move a growing sales team into software to manage leads (with unlimited users allowing scale) and then, once a contract is signed, pass it over into a more robust CRM for management/fulfillment/billing, and then move it back once the project is closed for ongoing sales and marketing outreach. That being said, I believe that 90 percent of you would see immediate value in a solution called GHL.

My agency was first introduced to GHL in November 2022 and since then we've moved more than twenty companies from other software solutions like JobNimbus, ClickUp, Monday, Zoho, Salesforce, Netsuite, HubSpot, even Excel/GoogleSheets into GHL with great success. The key reason is that GHL has a pricing model that is fair to business owners of all sizes. It's also considered a software as a service (SaaS) model solution (pay-as-you-go) and offers reseller options with a single pricing model that includes unlimited users, unlimited features, and unlimited contacts. What's the catch? There are some small usage fees to acquire toll-free or new tracking numbers, or to send out emails/texts beyond the credits that the platform offers. These nominal fees are far less or in line with all other email marketing and call tracking solutions. They seem fair and flexible—you pay more when you use more, and credits roll over. Also, unlike companies, such as Salesforce, that charge each company to customize the backend for features they want, GHL is constantly updating their platform and, when they do, they apply upgrades to all users. Everyone benefits. They provide a solution that is not "gating"; it's open, feature rich, and easy to use. GHL also includes the most popular features for sales and marketing, including:

- Texting, email, RVM (RingLessVoicemail): you can record a message and it bypasses the customer's ring on their device and goes straight to voicemail.
- Call Tracking and Call Recording: in-bound and out-bound.
- Calendar/Email integrations with Gmail/Outlook/iCloud/ Zoom and round-robin booking options.

Workflows that allow us to control the marketing mix based on the source of the lead. Example: where did it originate from, what stage in the pipeline is it currently in, and how long or how many days has it been in that status. Then, we can trigger texts, emails, ringless voicemails, and other automations like assigning or tagging a team member to follow up by placing a call in their queue.

- You can ask for reviews and manage replies in Google/ Facebook.
- Social media scheduling on GoogleMyBusiness, Facebook, Instagram, LinkedIn, TikTok, X, etc.
- Surveys, reporting, billing options with Quickbooks/Stripe integrations.

There's more, but this gives you an idea of the features that will add value for your specific needs. The platform boasts that companies can save over $7k a month from making the switch, as these integrations replace the need for a long list of third-party solutions like Calendly, Hatch, Podium, Birdeye, HubSpot, Hootsuite, Buffer, SurveyMonkey, or MailChimp.

GHL offers three levels: starter, unlimited, and at the very top is the reseller model, SaaS, which offers businesses a way to scale up quickly and share their knowledge with others in the same industry, creating ongoing residual revenue. Business owners simply upgrade their unlimited plan to turn on Stripe subscriptions and off you go.

Now that you have a flexible CRM that will help you track and manage your leads, the next step is to create a sales strategy that will support your marketing along the purchase funnel. Yes, the purchase funnel is back, but now we need to think about it starting again post-lead creation in the CRM. To recap with an example:

ROOFING MARKETING'S JOB: LEADS BABY!	
AWARENESS	My roof is getting old, I can see shingles missing. I might need to get it fixed.
CONSIDERATION	Hurricane season is right around the corner, I'd better look into a replacement.
INTENT	I am going to actively start looking for a roofing company near me by searching online.
ACTION	I am requesting a free quote online or calling a roofing company to schedule a site inspection.

ROOFING SALES' JOB: THEY CLOSE THE DEAL	
AWARENESS	Messaging that makes our company the right choice: products, warranty, reviews. Your leverageable points of difference!
CONSIDERATION	Compared to other proposals the customer received, we are better because of these reasons, or maybe we sweeten the deal with a discount or promotional offer.
INTENT	Verbal commitment from the homeowner, they received financing, insurance will cover the cost, or they can pay out of pocket for the new roof/repair.
ACTION	They signed a contract. We're ordering equipment and scheduling the crew.

HOW DO YOU BUILD A SALES FUNNEL TO SUPPORT MARKETING?

It's all about speed-to-lead. This means that once you ingest a lead, you have automations in place to reach out to that customer as fast as possible across multiple touch points. My recommendation is to send a text and email within five minutes of receiving the lead. Then, depending on the time of day, the customer should receive a call. If the first call is unanswered, call again (we call this a double dial), leaving a voicemail on the second attempt introducing your brand and the reason for the call. "Hi (customer name), it's (company name), I'm following up on your request to learn more about (solution), please give us a call back. Or you can schedule your own follow-up appointment by using the link we have sent you via text and email. We look forward to hearing from you."

Having a solid outreach process is critical to move the customer forward from lead to qualified. At Covert, we use the following key milestones for most organizations in their sales pipeline, but these may vary, depending on your industry:

- *Lead*—no appointment booked.
- *Qualified*—appointment booked, invitation sent to customer with Zoom/address. Email/text confirming appointment sent twenty-four hours before appointment, final text four hours before with instructions on how to reschedule via link, text, or to request a call from the team.
- *No Show/Cancel*—this status is only used in the event that the customer "ghosts" the salesman. No text, call, or email. Once this stage is set, we send automatic texts and emails with messaging ("sorry we missed you") and links to rebook the

appointment with the same salesman or on a company master calendar, depending on the client's unique workflows. We also queue up a manual call daily for up to fourteen days and start weekly drip emails on day 7 if the lead remains in this status.

- *Working*—this means that the original meeting time did not occur, but the customer was in touch with the company and requested to amend the time/day. When this happens, it's most likely that the current salesman will have the best chance of rebooking the appointment via direct communication with the customer over the next fourteen days. Post-fourteen days, if they still can't get a time confirmed, this lead should be sent to a call center and placed into a text/email nurture to stay top of mind.

- *Proposal shared*—this means that the meeting occurred and your team was able to present solutions and a quote for next steps. If the record does not move out of this status for seven days, we move it automatically to "nudge" for the salesman. Oftentimes we also recommend sending out a survey to the customer thirty minutes after the change in status for feedback on the customer's sales experience. If the results are one to three stars, we use automation to tag a sales manager for review. Additional automation may include a "thank-you" text to the customer twelve hours after the status changes followed by additional follow-up text on day 3 with a link to book a short follow-up meeting to review the proposal and answer any questions.

- *Nudge*—once the record moves either by salesman or automation, the system sends out an email to the customer from the salesman thanking them for meeting with them, reminding them about our company's leverageable points of difference, and concluding with a link to book a follow-up meeting. A similar short text is sent followed by an additional follow-up three days later if the contact remains in Nudge status. On day 5, if we have not heard back from the customer, drip emails start—one per week for the first eight weeks, and then one every two weeks up to 365 days later.

- *Limbo*—this status is used to "park" a contact (lead) for whatever reason. For example, let's say the customer says they will be traveling in France for the next three weeks. The salesman would then move them from "proposal shared" to "limbo," leave notes on the reason, and create a task reminding them to follow up on X date. In the Limbo category, we set the nurture drip emails to send 1× per month with the intention of staying top of mind with the customer but not overbearing, which can result in unsubscribes.

- *Nurture*—this status immediately starts the 1× 8-week drips/2× ongoing drips. It should be started when the customer goes dark after a series of outreach efforts by the salesman. This includes three texts, voicemails, and emails from the salesman. I can't stress enough the importance of every salesman leaving detailed notes on the record in the CRM for outreach efforts. When using GHL, all three of these efforts are clearly tracked inside of each contact record, making it easy for management to track efforts.

- *Verbal commitment*—if the contact gets "stuck" in this status for over fourteen days, nurture drip emails/texts start and a tag is created for leadership to escalate and assess why the contact failed to convert.

- *Contract signed*—once the contract is signed, an immediate thank-you email/text is sent via automation from the salesman to the customer. On day 2, we ask for our first review ("How did we do selling you this solution?") and include a reward like a $10 Amazon gift card for every channel on which a review is posted (Google, Facebook, Yelp, etc.). Then finally on day 3 we recommend sending an email introducing the next steps in the customer's journey, that is, what to expect, and asking for referrals urging the customer to join a referral program by downloading an app or generating a referral link, etc.

- *DQ*—This stands for disqualified and should include the reason. I like to break these into two categories: yes and no. Yes DQs should be added to a nurture drip. No DQs should never be contacted again.
  - □ Yes examples—Not interested right now, stopped contact, failed credit, etc.
  - □ No examples—Bad contact info, out of scope, out of territory, not able to provide service, asked to be removed from list, etc.
- *Post Solution*—depending on the industry, once the project is closed out, a final survey should be sent to the customer. If the survey receives four to five stars, through automation we move the customer to a status = "post review" and ask once again for them to review us online for a reward. If the survey results were one to three stars, the contact is moved to a status "follow-up required" and tagged to leadership for further review.

It's also important to note that each unique lead source should have its own expectations and process for sales outreach. If the lead was "self-generated" by a salesman, there should not be automations sent out by the company to "book an appointment" and paid lead sources should also contain references to the company of origin to increase open rates, that is, email subject "Best Company (lead source) & (company name)—Schedule Your Free (service) Consultation Today!" Whatever CRM you use, ensure that you are classifying each source and have the ability to curate workflows and messaging to create the best user experience.

I know what you may be thinking: My sales team won't use this tool. We already have a process that works. Why rock the boat? But remember, these tools will increase lead to sale rates by 20 percent or more and help ensure that every lead is controlled to some extent. We know that customers received (or didn't) the drip/text emails stating approved brand messaging (we know this from the delivery and open rate of each message). If your sales team pushes back, it's time for them to find another job. This is your business and the future requires transparent communication, meaning we can see and analyze each team member's efforts while engaging with customers. Automations and sales expectations also make it easier to identify lead quality by source. If everyone is doing the same things, in the same ways, trends in lead quality are easy to spot. If everyone is managing leads on their own, marketing will never be able to truly assess the value of lead source A versus B.

Lastly, you might be asking yourself, "How do I get the leads from my website or lead providers into the CRM?" Solutions like Zapier exist for a monthly fee that allow users with no code knowledge to connect systems. For companies that engage with an agency or developer, you should include the integration in the SOW from the start. At Covert, we use a proprietary solution called MANA (themanasolution.com), which in Hawaiian means power, and we connect clients systems through Application Program Interfaces (APIs) that allow systems to connect to each other. This means more customization opportunities and no ongoing costs. There are also paid website plug-ins that can be used to map records into your desired CRM. Another popular option is to create the form from within the CRM and then pop it onto your site using an inline frame (iframe). An iframe is an HTML element that loads another HTML page within your page. It's important to note that they are hosted from the parent site and not within our control, which means they can't be styled (or designed to be pretty or match your website theme). This also impacts your ability to track conversions, as the record fires or "submits" inside of the iframe, which means it's outside of your website. It's for this reason that we never like to use iframes but, depending on your selected CRM, there might be valid use cases.

 ANNA'S TIP

Make sure your website leads and paid vendor leads go directly into your CRM and are not received via email. Lead providers should be able to use webhooks, web-to-lead forms, Zapier, or custom scripts to create leads directly into your CRM and pass over the required fields: name, email, phone, address, notes, appointment day/time, lead source, and assign it to the correct user on your team for next steps. If you're using WordPress as your website framework, ALWAYS install CRM backup (a free plug-in) that will serve as a backup for all form submissions. Redundancy is key online. It's best practice to be a little paranoid (technology breaks) and make sure you never lose a lead.

Now that you have the right website, best CRM, and way to manage all your leads through automation, let's talk about how to determine what a customer is worth so you can set the correct budget and attribution metrics to track your campaign's effectiveness post-launch.

01000011 011011
01101111 01100100 01100101 001000
001000
01101111 011000
01101111 01100100 011001
01101111 011000
01101111 01100110 00100000

CHAPTER FOUR

HOW MUCH IS A NEW CUSTOMER WORTH?

The problem with worth is that it can change on a dime. Just like currency, the value is perceived and fluctuates based on factors like GDP or inflation. Changes to your customer's value can be the result of your business model shifting, or directly tied to how you quantify the "lifetime" value of a customer. Depending on your industry, expectations must be set before starting any marketing campaign, otherwise overspending will occur.

I like to identify a customer's worth in two parts: 1. Initial contract value or average cart price. 2. Lifetime value of that customer, which consists of recurring revenue potential services, like software, subscriptions, professional services, upsell opportunities, and referrals. For example, if you are selling a commodity like tissues, the initial value of a new customer buying a box isn't much, but the lifetime value of a loyal customer who will purchase the Kleenex brand over the next twenty years adds up. Then, if we consider adding a new wholesale account or distribution channel, the value of that new customer is much greater.

Determining your customer's worth directly relates to your objective task budget and creates benchmarks to evaluate your marketing mix. To determine the value, the first step is to ask yourself a few questions and separate them by each product or service offering (such as homeowners, business owners, single customers, wholesale customers).

- How much money does my company make when we sign a new customer—before and after the costs of running the business (gross revenue versus net revenue)?
- Will that customer be recurring and by what frequency—daily, monthly, quarterly?
- Is that customer going to refer me, and what are the number of times they will—1×, 3×, 5×?
- Next, you look at your current statistics and outline your desired growth goals.
- Of all the leads we acquire, what percentage will turn into customers by service offering?
- How much do we want to make this year from each service?

For example, if we were selling cars, a dealer might determine that a new customer is worth on average $10,000 per car sold. The likelihood of the customer buying a car in the future is high, as most customers are loyal to a brand. So, we may predict a sale every five to ten years (or three with a lease). It's fairly unlikely that they will refer a friend without a strong referral program in place. But if there is one, what percentage of customers will refer a friend? To simplify this for your planned marketing, let's just look at hard metrics for cost to acquire that first-time customer.

When analyzing our conversion rates, let's assume that, out of twenty appointments, we sell five cars. That means our conversion rate is 25 percent appointment-to-sale. If our annual goal was to make $3 million, we would need to sell 300 cars, which would require 1,200 appointments. How much are we willing to spend in marketing to achieve this desired goal? Let's say we are willing to spend 3 percent or $90,000 of the $3 million. That breaks down into $7,500 per month—so that then should become our budget, right? WRONG. One of the biggest mistakes that clients make is spreading their budget evenly over a fiscal calendar.

 ANNA'S TIP

Your online marketing budget should be fluid, which means that you have spending goals by month or quarter, but will only spend what you must. If you don't spend it all in the outlined month, it should roll over into the following month to meet online changes in demand. Sometimes this also means spending far more during key demand periods.

This boils down to a concept called "the threshold of indifference," which directly relates to impression share and critical mass messaging. If your company is not targeting the right audience with enough impressions over a short period of time (frequency), then you will never be "relevant," and essentially will be wasting your money. An example might be a company that has an annual marketing budget of $60,000 and so allocates $5k per month, spreading it over a few initiatives: $2,000 in GoogleAds, $1,000 in social media, and $2,000 in radio. The result may be that they never build up enough impressions to their target audience to reach scale, essentially staying below the threshold of indifference. Their audience won't remember them.

Now, let's say we take that same budget and spend it on a single spot during the Super Bowl—boom! The reach is so massive that the brand is now above the threshold, and what we have determined is that, with just a small amount of maintenance marketing targeted at our now engaged audience, companies stay above the threshold. Although this example mentions traditional advertising, this same concept applies to digital advertising and should be carefully considered by industry to meet the desired results from your planned campaigns.

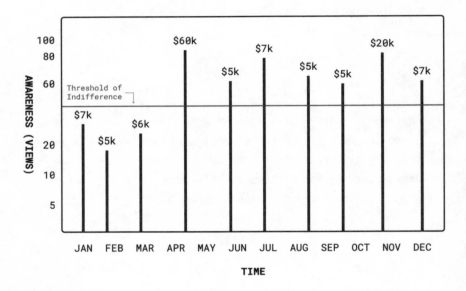

The next factor to consider is seasonality. If you sell more cars in Q4, then you'll want to make sure to support those trends with appropriate budget allocation for your digital marketing mix and update your expectations with new benchmarks for success. For example, out of the total appointments that run in Nov/Dec, do you still experience a 25 percent conversion rate or does it go up because there are end-of-year promos and the customer is more motivated?

Here is an example of what you are trying to create to set a baseline:

2024	LEADS	APPOINTMENTS (DEMO)	% LEAD TO DEMO	SALES	% DEMO TO SALE
Q1	300	40	13%	10	25%
Q2	300	40	13%	10	25%
Q3	300	80	27%	30	38%
Q4	500	110	22%	50	45%
Total	1400	270	19%	100	37%

Next is to determine what you spent on marketing to achieve your current benchmarks. If in 2023 we spent $80,000 to generate the 1,400 leads, that would break out into $57.14 price-per-lead, $296 cost-per-appointment, and a cost-per-sale of $800. So, if our goal is to increase sales in 2024 from 100 cars to 300 cars with a spend of $90,000, then we need to get our lead costs down, and then hopefully, using sales automations, appointment rates go up. With some simple math we can determine that our team would require approximately 4,250 leads (annual) to book 807 appointments, of which we would close 300 deals at the current appointment-to-sale rate. That would bring our cost-per-lead to $21, cost-per-appointment to $111, and cost-per-sale to $300. Now that you have a baseline, you must ask yourself whether your projections are crazy or whether you can achieve your desired results with the current media budget. Let's find out!

The next step is to analyze your website's traffic to determine which sources were responsible for the leads you generated. This brings us to the concept of attribution, which is how we assign credit to our traffic sources.

WHAT IS ATTRIBUTION?

In marketing, everyone wants to take credit for your lead. It's easier to do this online versus offline. In digital marketing, we use the concept of attribution to give and take credit for user's actions that occur after interacting with an ad. Attribution comes in all shapes and sizes and is one of the most critical pieces when understanding the customer's journey. Until recently, the most common and default attribution was "last click," which meant that the media source would "take credit" if they showed the ad that resulted in the customer's last click before they converted on your website, typically over a thirty-day window of time. Some companies, even Google Ads, will set default conversion windows to ninety days on the new G4 Analytics model. In fact, I have worked with some top-funnel media companies that go as far as to attempt to take credit for traffic that converted 120 days later. That is just absurd! But let's start with a simple example.

Let's say we are a real estate company focused on driving new home purchases. We launched a Google Ads search campaign and started serving search ads. A potential homeowner searches for "low-price two-bedroom condo near me," and up pops our ad. The user clicks and arrives at our website and searches for condos for several minutes, but does not create an account or request a showing. They then leave the site, and we follow them with relevant remarketing ads of additional two-bedroom condos that match their search criteria. They see one that looks interesting, click and arrive at that listing, but still do not request a showing. They leave for a second time; now they're on Facebook scrolling through the feed when we serve another ad with that latest two-bedroom condo listing with which they had engaged earlier. They click one more time and finally, on this visit, sign up for a free account and request a showing, resulting in a hard conversion.

Now the real estate company owner is looking at a monthly report, and from the data, it looks like they had three conversions: one from search (Google), one from remarketing, and one from Facebook, but they didn't. They had one conversion and all three media sources contributed to that lead. We want to know how many site visits (sessions), by source and how many days it took from the customer's first visit to conversion so that, when the boss says that we need more leads, we can divide the funds over our media mix sources appropriately to generate the greatest result. The problem is that, with so many partners and different types of reporting, it's hard to identify or assign value without a lot of manual digging. The most important thing is that all your media attribution is consistent across partners. My belief is that a media source deserves credit for what we call a view-through conversion only if it occurs within twenty-four hours after being served. Trying to take credit for showing a customer one ad impression that they didn't click on for thirty days, sixty days, or 120 days is ludicrous. Think about how many ads you see in one day. That's now how humans are programmed. The same is true with TV. We can associate lift in foot traffic or online website traffic when the spots are airing, but trying to attribute anything even a week after the last spot aired is tough.

We typically break these into what are called conversion paths and set some expectations. How many touches (i.e., site sessions by user) did it require us to move the customer from first visit to conversion? G4 Analytics organizes these into three buckets, which can be seen under the "advertising" tab as Early, Mid, and Late touch points, basically identifying which percentage of your traffic was responsible for taking credit on that conversion. If you toggle from *data driven* to *last click,* you will see 100 percent of your traffic in the Late Touchpoints column. This means that traffic source was the last one the customer took before resulting in a site conversion. Data driven fairly attributes traffic across other channels (paid, social, organic), which tells you that your customer came back multiple times before taking that final action. You can scroll down on the page to see the average length of time or number to touchpoints as they relate to each traffic source for further insights.

COVERT CODE ATTRIBUTION RULES

These are my recommendations for how to measure media types fairly:

- *Remarketing:* One-day view-through thirty-day click (meaning that if a customer clicked on your ad and returned within thirty days organically and converted, we can take credit).
- *Search Marketing:* Thirty-day data driven or position based. That means we are giving credit to every click that might have happened during the conversion window. It is incredibly important to drill down to what your true cost-per-lead was. For example, let's say we are selling home loans, and each click on Google costs $15, and over the period of thirty days it took three clicks for the same user to finally convert. If you were using last-click attribution, it might look like the cost to acquire this customer was just $15 from Google, but the truth is that your CPA was $45. A big difference, wouldn't you say?

Position based or now data driven (better) gives credit to every click throughout the customer's journey and can also allow us to gauge the length of time it takes for a customer to convert. If the customer clicked once and then, forty-five days later, they clicked again and converted, each of those clicks would get a .5 conversion credit in Google Ads because it happened over the desired attribution range (the first one over the first thirty days, the second over the next thirty days) and that then indicates that our customer's journey was longer. If this continues to happen, we eventually will conclude that our customer's average time from first visit to conversion is forty-five days. This learning is critical for your media budget. If it takes forty-five days to convert a customer with two clicks, creating budgets and predictions for achieving results needs to change to reflect that. Otherwise, a company might cut its budget too soon and miss out on the win. For example, if you spent $20k in June and didn't see the desired results and then only allocated $10k in July, essentially reducing your impression share and ability to win that second click, your chances of winning decrease or disappear.

- *Front-Funnel/Programmatic:* one-day view or thirty-day click.
- *Social Media:* Thirty-day click or from viewing an assisted conversions report in Google Analytics.

 ANNA'S TIP

Before hiring a media company to conduct an online campaign on your behalf ask them what their attribution model is. If their answer is anything besides thirty-day or seven-day click and twenty-four-hour view-through, run for the hills.

SETTING UP CONVERSIONS AND ATTRIBUTION IN G4 ANALYTICS

There are a plethora of ways you can use the new G4 Analytics to find out how traffic is getting to your site (from what source), which landing pages they are looking at, where they are physically located, and which devices they're using. My recommendation is to not get too bogged down in the details, as data changes quickly. You might not have been doing it right from the start, so why cry over spilled milk? What's important is to make sure you know how to assess future results, and that starts with tracking your hard/soft goals so you can determine the total conversion rate by source after the campaigns deploy. One thing that WILL be very upsetting or a nuisance for many readers is that, in July 2023, Google Analytics stopped reporting on UA—Universal Analytics and now only supports G4. In many instances, Google may have migrated your account into a new G4 tag stream but that is not always the case. That means that while you thought your site was tracking behavior, it might not be.

If you have access to your Google Analytics, login now. If you see this banner at the top, you need to complete the migration by following the instructions. Or you can also click the button to "automatically set up a basic Google Analytics 4 Property." Once you get access to your new G4 property, you want to make sure that you see a green bar under "setup assistant" that confirms your data is following.

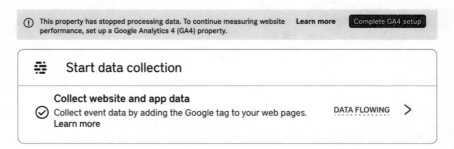

The second thing to mention is that the way conversions are tracked is different from it was before. In the UA version we called them "goals," and in G4 they are created as events, and a business owner must manually mark each event as a conversion to be included in the top-level report. When you login for the first time, you will see that Google has created some automatic events for you, such as first_visit, page_view, scroll, session_start, view_search_results, click, and purchase. You will need to create new events for both your hard and soft conversions as previously identified, and then flip on the "track as conversion," keeping in mind that until a user does complete that event, you will not be able to see it on the conversion reporting. The easiest way to track conversions for those without technical knowledge is by using a thank-you page or destination URL, meaning that any time someone submits a free quote form, the user will redirect to a page/free-quote/thank-you and when they arrive at the location, track it as a conversion.

As G4 setups are always complex, please consult the resource section of *thecovertcode.com* for instructions and videos. In that same resource section, you will also learn about setting attribution, and you'll want to make sure that you are tracking "paid and organic channels" and click-through conversions thirty days and all other conversions events thirty days (they will tell you ninety days is recommended, but that limits your ability to analyze marketing budgets).

SETTING THE BASELINE

Assuming that you have data reporting and conversions tracking, the easiest way to set a baseline is to go to G4 and click on reports/user acquisition (edit) and add to metrics "session conversion rate" into your view. You will see a breakout of all types of traffic by channel group and be able to filter by different key metrics. You want to know the number of users, engaged sessions (those are the users who stayed on your site and didn't bounce), and then total conversions and session conversion rate. In the chart, you'll see some terms that will help you quickly navigate deeper and also relate directly to setting up UTMs, which will help answer basic questions about your web traffic. When logging into G4, you will be able to filter and organize data by the following dimensions: channel, source, medium, campaign, and platform.

DEFAULT CHANNEL GROUP	This will show you traffic to your site broken out by channel: paid search, display, direct, organic search, organic social, referral, and unassigned traffic types.
MEDIUM (UTM_MEDIUM)	Medium helps you determine the type of media your campaign is using: CPC, display, email, referral.
SOURCE (UTM_SOURCE)	This is the domain the user came from before arriving at your site. A source could be Google, Bing, Google My Business, Facebook, Yahoo, or could indicate where the content was published, such as MailChimp.
CAMPAIGN NAME (UTM_CAMPAIGN)	This is the name of your campaign, product, or promo code. Be as descriptive as possible (winterholidaysale2023 versus holidaysale).
OTHERS— CAMPAIGN CONTENT (UTM_CONTENT) AND TERM (UTM_TERM)	These potential fields can be used to identify paid search keywords or differentiate ads or links that point to the same domain for A/B testing.

As you fiddle with your G4 report, make sure you are selecting a "hard conversion" to track in the drop-down, reviewing each independently (i.e., change "All events" to view the hard metric or free quote). If you include all events into conversions, they will include soft metrics and preadded events like scroll or click, and this will not provide you with an accurate way to understand if you will be able to achieve your desired lead goals from your marketing budget. One of the easiest tools to appropriately assign value to traffic is to use "Urchine Tracking Module" or UTM tracking parameters in every paid campaign.

CREATING UTM TRACKING

Every single paid ad you have on any partner's website or through any company should contain a UTM tracking parameter so that you can give credit correctly for traffic and sales generated from your third-party provider to your site. And if they're so wonderful, they should mandate that you have tracking (or add it as a default) as it is one of the easiest ways to prove and take credit for a direct visit to a conversion event. Don't get crazy. UTMs only work on the *same* user's journey or site visit. So, if a customer clicks on your ad in Google, visits your site for the first time, leaves before buying, and then comes back from seeing your remarketing ad or organically on their own, the UTM for Google will not be there, but yes, your Google Ads campaign still deserves some credit.

 ANNA'S TIP

To generate a fast and dirty UTM, use a builder -> https://ga-dev-tools. google/campaign-url-builder/ and print out my Cheat Sheet to get started with naming hierarchy best practices.

FORECASTING

Now that we have an idea of our total site traffic conversion rate, let's make some assumptions. Last year we generated 1,400 leads at a

1 percent total site conversion rate from 140,000 first-time visitors. Readers, this is important. G4 has lots of settings and it can get confusing fast to disseminate total traffic conversion rates by engaged users and drill down into those "hard conversions." I recommend that you don't get caught up in the details. Look at the total first-time visitors (all traffic sources) and then just assume that 50 percent are engaged. Then look at the total number of leads you have in your system and get your total first-time-visit to hard conversion rate. Once you become an expert and have a year of historical data, you can really start to dive deeper, but for most companies this isn't a valuable use of time and, as data and trends change quickly, you don't want to make decisions based on the past but rather use trends that you can control. If we want to triple our sales, we need to increase traffic or conversion rates. Assuming we could convert 2 or 3 percent of all traffic, that would put us into the right position to supply sales with leads that, looking at historical efforts, should yield the desired lift. Ok, sounds easy enough, right? The next step is to set a baseline of what is possible to achieve in terms of CPC and CPM impressions from each paid media source to ascertain if our set budgets will be able to yield the desired results or if we need to reset expectations. In the next chapter, we will review how your ads really work to prepare you to build a media mix and deploy your campaign.

 ANNA'S TIP

Create a company leads-goal for marketing and closed sales goals for sales. There will be ways to track leads by source, but it will never be pure because the customer's journey online and offline coexist (and the goal of both is to get the customer to arrive at your website). The only way to track a pure conversion from paid search is if it happens on the same visit.

                              01000011 011011
           01101111 01100100 01100101 001000
                                       001000
                    01101111 011001
           01101111 01100100 0110010
                    01101111 011001
  01101111 01100110 00100000

CHAPTER FIVE

HOW YOUR DIGITAL ADS ACTUALLY WORK

———

Like its name suggests, the web is a mystery of connections from point to point. How devices connect and display data can be confusing, sometimes intentionally so. But I want to help demystify this process. Let's start at the beginning. How do we cookie or identify a device, and what options are there to serve ads to that user?

HOW CAN YOU REACH A DEVICE?

There are several ways to locate and serve ads to a device, including Wi-Fi (50-yard range), Bluetooth (a few yards), and Radio Frequency (RF) or Airdrop, otherwise referred to as Beacon technology (30-yard range).

WI-FI

Every Wi-Fi router has an IP address that identifies the devices connected to it. Each device has characters added to the string of your primary IP that show association by router, so if my router was 192.168.86.1, my iPhone device IP is 192.168.86.22. Because multiple devices can be connected to the same IP address, that is your first "concern" when trying to identify a user and serve ads to that same person over cross-devices: computer, phone, and tablet. For example, let's say John has a wife and three kids all living at home. Together they have eight devices all associated with the same router IP address. So, we can't easily use that IP to associate interests because John is looking at vacations and his wife is interested in fiction books and the kids all have unique interests and online behaviors. The challenge increases when you have a large office building with 200+ users with 600+ devices. It's for this reason that most systems will simply disregard IP associations since they are not trustworthy or usable.

APPS

Similarly, every time you delete an app, redownload, or sign in again, even using the same email and password, a new fingerprint ID is created. The historical data from the last fingerprint is removed. The only useful piece of information that can create association or a user match is collected from a user's session that started from the same browser on which it was initially created, meaning that we are able to determine without a reasonable doubt that this is the same user and they're back for more. As a result, simply knowing the email address of the customer we want to target isn't enough, not unless you have so much cookie saturation online that you can reassociate that user's new login or visits across multiple sessions and devices. Publishers like Google, Quantcast, and Criteo have millions of pixels out there. It might take some time, but eventually they would have the ability to reassociate your current session with a tag and add you back into an audience for display targeting. That is, of course, if it was from a computer that logged a specific domain cookie.

What about mobile devices? If the domain you visit on your mobile device does not contain the www (www.domainname.com), but rather just domainname.com, the cookies created from that session are temporary instead of permanent. The www. is the C name folder on the domain that stores all the assets. If the site does not have www. before it, the folder is located somewhere on the root and under the hood (within the file) of the C name. For example, if the site was app.mydomain.com, then the app. would be the C name and location of the assets. So, assuming your mobile user does go to the www. yourdomain.com link that session, it will be stored as permanent. But that's really not forever. We assume long term that sessions will refresh (every time you visit that domain, the clock starts over) and inactivity after 90–120 days usually results in a cleaning or purge of the cookie. That's why, if you go back to a site that you haven't been to for a while, it will ask you to login again. The session memory has expired. This process is good for the consumer because it protects your device from being hacked, but it's not ideal for advertisers who assume that they can target a customer for 90+ days.

The question for me becomes, "How long does it take to establish the relink?" That goes back to saturation; the more pixels a partner has, the faster the AI can connect the dots. When a temporary cookie is created, it is valid for seven to fourteen days or based on a user's system setup. Once they log out and then log back in, any old sessions will be cleaned out and a new token will be created for the next login. But what about single-session logins, you might ask? Those work by allowing us to verify with 100 percent accuracy that all these devices belong to the same person. This is done by keeping track of each cookie or session created via a central database and combining those cookies and sessions on the back end. The most typical way to login, however, is with multi-login, which directly impacts your ability to identify a single user over multiple devices with accuracy.

THE GRAY ZONE

I'm sure every reader has been to an airport or Starbucks and, before being able to join the Wi-Fi network, you arrive at a screen that asks you to enter the password and accept terms. That is the critical step to being able to hijack or control users' sessions. By first signing into this "cover page," you're giving the Wi-Fi owner the control of your device. They can show you whatever they want. That includes taking over display ads, sending push notifications, and yes, if you watch those hacker movies, that is how they can manipulate search. In this scenario, they establish the "first session access" of the target's device, then when the user goes to Google and searches for something, that service delivers results that look just like Google but, in fact, are from hacker.google.com, allowing them to change the results and present the search criteria that they want you to see. It could be validating that a person does work for that company, has a net worth of $2 billion, attended this school, has won these awards, etc. Scary, huh? That's why you should always delete and reinstall apps every few months (Facebook, Instagram, Chrome), and when you prepare to board your flight, clear your cache or turn off all your devices so you won't be the victim of any sneaky spoofing.

Legal spoofing is possible and can be used to control and distribute advertising based on location. Once the user accepts the terms of a Wi-Fi connection, the Wi-Fi router becomes the CDN (content delivery network) and, as long as the user is accessing the internet on that session, it can deliver their ad content as the customer clicks from site to site. It's a way to force those "open inventory slots" on the display network to be filled with ad messages. I have yet to experience any company doing this well, which always surprises me, especially at large airports like LAX or Zurich. It would be an ideal way to drive duty-free sales, flight upgrades, or other types of airport services to an active on-premises audience.

RF/BEACON

A much more trustworthy tool to tag a user based on location is via RF or beacon. This works by establishing a connection with any device that is within range. The catch? That user has to accept the message. Apple's AirDrop feature is a type of beacon and works the same way. Even if you are sending yourself pictures or a file from one device to the other, you still have to accept that information for your protection. Bluetooth is similar; you must be within a few yards of the connection and then it is accepted. Once established, advertisers can send push notifications to your phone through an application... but can't serve you an ad on the display network. Why? Because they are different entry points —> in-app versus online.

HOW DO ADS GET DISTRIBUTED IN THE AD EXCHANGE?

To distribute content online a CDN is used that essentially is a network of servers located in geographic regions that pay internet providers to display content to the online user. In digital advertising there are two parts, a seller who we collectively refer to as publishers or an ad buyer referred to as advertisers. Advertisers can include product manufacturers, service providers, third-party ad agencies, intermediary ad networks, etc. The easiest way to break this up is into sell-side inventory and buy-side demand.

Each publisher must create or hire a CDN and then, on behalf of website publishers, distribute ads to consumers. How this actually happens is unknown to the public and largely controlled by Google,[6] which is the subject of a lawsuit from the Justice Department which sued Google for monopolizing digital advertising technologies.

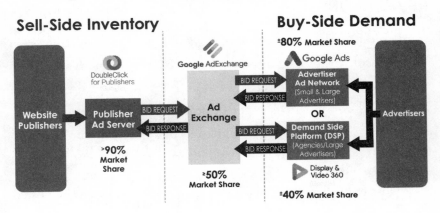

What we believe is happening is that, depending on time of year, audience targeting, bid strategy, and content type, our ads will be shown to people physically located in the target area we have identified and "won" based on a bid from the live auction. But how can we prove that a purchased impression from a CDN did in fact run on the desired website publishers' site, app, etc.? The answer is you can't because they don't want you to know. When uploading ads to a publisher like AdRoll, Google, or Microsoft, they are asking you to

6   "Justice department sues Google for monopolizing digital advertising technologies," Office of Public Affairs, Department of Justice, January 24, 2023, https://www.justice.gov/opa/pr/justice-department-sues-google-monopolizing-digital-advertising-technologies.

essentially host the creative from their platform and then serve those ads to customers over some "behind the curtain" CDN.

Here's an example: When you see an ad on the display network, right click on it and select "copy image address" and then paste it into a new URL window, you will see a string in the domain address that will appear with a masked URL destination of the ad delivered.

If you then take that same string and do a Google search for the file, you will see that it does not exist. Or, you will see references to the ad exchange publisher that it came from, that is, Criteo, Google, Adsense, etc. The result? An unbiased third party is not able to verify that the impression ran because every time the publisher serves the ad, the URL is different or masked, thus creating a dark web of missing links. The only way to get around this is for you to host your own ad content, creating your own CDN, then allow that publisher to distribute it through their channels but pull the assets from a single library (that you can control). Then you'll know that the ad was viewed this many times and was clicked on by this many users.

Most publishers don't make it easy or allow creative to be hosted outside of their platform. There are some publishers who do allow advertisers to host creative outside of their platform (like Criteo and Quantcast) and others, like StackAdapt, who will even allow an impression pixel to be easily added into your creative to double prove that it did in fact run. Publishers that can be trusted also use third-party tools that monitor ad security and validate traffic, such as Boltive and Moat. Boltive provides oversight for ad security, meaning that they scan ad creative looking for "bad ads" that distribute viruses, cheat or scam end users, or are offensive in nature. Did you know that today ad creative is one of the easiest ways to infect and spread malware? You don't need to click on the ad to be infected; all that is required is for it to run on your device as you enjoy browsing web or in-app content. On the other side of the spectrum are companies like Oracle Moat, a third party that provides ad measurement and a marketing analytics suite designed to help advertisers, publishers, and platforms measure media performance across the breadth of their digital and TV advertising campaigns with features including IVT reports to measure real human versus bot clicks, viewability, and other advanced attention metrics that reveal how consumers are engaging with your ads across channels and devices. The important thing to remember is while these services exist they're still "services" and must be subscribed to by your media publisher. This means that there is no way to validate impression share or click authenticity from an unbiased third party, such as Nielsen for TV, Scarborough for radio, etc.

THE PLOT THICKENS: AD STACKING AND CLICK BUBBLES

Ad stacking is essentially when multiple ads are served on top of one another inside of the display container, that is, code reference div. container. The initial intent of this concept was non-malicious and was to help prove to advertisers that the media company was able to target ads to customers they cared about. The catch? Your ad wasn't served because the customer left the page before it had the *opportunity* to display. As an example: The customer landed on yahoo.com and then, within five seconds (or the average time for an animated display ad to go through its rotation), they scrolled down the page. If your company's ad was next up on the queue (after the first ad ran), that meant that it was not billable but had the opportunity to show. With this information, the media company could prove that targeting was valid and then tried to get advertisers to spend more for the first position. What ended up happening was that unethical publishers charged for impressions that were "delivered." It was on the page in the div.container, but not "viewed." That, mixed together with "click bubbles," can drastically impact advertisers' or media publishers' online results. A single click on the domain can ripple and impact more than the single button or layer that the customer selected. So, for example, if the website publisher or domain.com on the display network wanted to increase results, they could sell the same display space to multiple CDNs. Then, if a customer clicked on one ad, it would balloon down and up, showing a click on every ad delivered on the page, even those not yet viewable to the end user. The result: impression numbers are not correct and neither are clicks, because your browser will open each behind the curtain with the power of JavaScript. Scary, huh? It's easy to see when additional content is on a domain by inspecting the element (view source code on the page), and the appropriate way to charge for an impression would be only when the div = display: view.

All things considered, the biggest head scratcher is trying to identify potential fraud in this type of situation, as the ad delivery network, partner display site, and browser all have ways to influence actions and fabricate data. To create a safe space, it's imperative that rules are implemented to protect all parties, but how? The answer is…I'm not sure we will ever find a solution, until the media giants agree to open up their skirt and divulge the mysteries of ad distribution along the display network. Because I think we can all agree that it is better for the industry to self-regulate than to be overregulated! In the short term, there are partners out there who are trustworthy and deliver easy-to-verify results that increase campaign ROI and ensure that ads are clicked on by humans versus bots and that impressions were viewed or heard.

THE BATTLE OF THE BOTS

It was April of 2021 when I was first introduced to ClickCease, a Telavi-based company that protects ad campaigns from bot clicks across Google Ads, Microsoft, and Facebook. At the time, I had been struggling to find a solution to the rapid and noticeable declines in search and social campaign performance (i.e., total traffic to conversion rates), and was panicked as to what the reason might be. How could all our paid conversion traffic decline industry-wide in just six to eight months? Could customer behavior have shifted so drastically and, if so, what did that mean for our allocation of the media mix? I spent hours sifting through data and trying to figure out how to reverse the trends before clients started to pull spend and lose confidence.

That's when I stumbled upon a ClickCease ad mentioning that 27 percent of all online paid traffic was fake. I was intrigued as that number aligned with my clients' decline in results and started a fourteen-day free trial. I was quickly impressed with the ease of setup, including a no-code-required WordPress plug-in as well as clear instructions for clients on Shopify/BigCommerce to add the code to tag manager or directly into the site header. The next step was to integrate Google Ads and Facebook (also a quick one-step process). Within seven days, I saw the results start to add up. My campaign metrics went back up to historical norms and my clients were saving big money, 40 percent on average, across connected protected paid digital accounts.

So, the next question you might be asking yourself is, who is responsible for all this fake traffic? The truth is that while competitors may be clicking on ads, the biggest contributor is from our media partners, who are deploying bots to click on their own ads, increasing revenue and inflating numbers to win more ad budgets from advertisers. Yikes! There is also the concept of threshold protection, which means that we don't want the same user to click multiple times on our ad, which can also increase spend at a reduced conversion rate (i.e., they have already been to our site and now we want to pass the ball to remarketing to take it the rest of the way), which is more effective and cheaper than paid search (more on that in chapter 8). Threshold protection allows us to set minimums by length of time since the target user's last click, allowing advertisers to feel greater confidence in spending more per click to generate new traffic versus potentially showing up multiple times to the same user during their online research "intent" phase, increasing costs and decreasing results. Depending on your company's industry, different tolerance levels are recommended by the platform. Some examples: detect and block an IP if they click on an ad two times within ten minutes, or allow three clicks within seven days.

Important things to know about ClickCease:

- Google Ads has a real-time integration with ClickCease and automatically blocks bots right inside the platform, resulting in a dramatic reduction of budgets (around 30 percent).

- Microsoft Ads does not offer a direct integration with Click-Cease and, as a result, advertisers are required to manually add negative IPs into each campaign's settings. The problem is that Microsoft only allows one hundred negatives per campaign at any given time. What we have found is that, in some cases, hundreds of negative IPs can be blocked a day. The good news is that, in 2023, ClickCease introduced "cross-domain" and "cross-platform" blocking, meaning that if you are an agency and have multiple domains being monitored, you can automatically block IPs across all protected domains in your account, as well as add them to a negative IP list of up to 500 at a time with refreshing capability and can include an IP range exclusion. Once this setting was added, we immediately saw our Microsoft campaigns return to normal conversion rates. Cross platform would be the better setting for individual companies, and means that if you block an IP address from a Google Ad it would automatically block from Facebook.

- Facebook protection must be manually turned on by each campaign or by boosted ad post created. The average saved on agency FB campaigns is 40–50 percent, so this is dramatic. Remember, this protection only works if you are sending traffic to a URL on your domain. Running FB ads that go to a lead form inside the platform will not be protected.

Another important thing to mention is that ClickCease only protects search campaigns and anything running through the display network or partner networks will not be protected. I discovered this in 2022 when Google came out with a type of campaign called "discovery" and "performance max" and I was intrigued. It sounded great and brought back one of my favorite strategies that offered advertisers a way to distribute ads to users who had free Gmail accounts (above their emails), a program that had been sunset several years before. So, the agency gave it a shot. The early results were incredible, but they didn't last. I was running a campaign for Get The Referral app when I got a ping on our client Slack channel. Something strange was happening with the conversions being reported; we didn't see them in HubSpot. I sprang into action, and logged into the client's Unbounce account, which was the program they were using at the time (before we custom-redesigned the site and brought all landing pages into HubSpot), and downloaded the submissions. It was immediately clear that bots were filling out the form. Out of 149 submissions, only eighteen were human. The rest were from companies like bozzcello. com, domani.com, armyspy.com; the list was long.

But how would that be possible if we had ClickCease? I opened up a chat with the platform and quickly learned that anything outside of Google Search (such as Display Network or Search Partners) was *not* protected. That was the end of that campaign (and all our performance max and discovery campaigns agency-wide). The same is true with YouTube, which is owned by Google. If you're going to run a campaign, factoring in this knowledge is key. Sometimes budgets are so big that you might not care that 20–30 percent of leads are fake, but my personal recommendation is to only use pre-roll video distribution from a trusted partner who will provide false click reports, proof of impression share, ability not to have ads skipped after they run for seven seconds, and if they do make an error, will take ownership! In the media, we say that you're only as good as your last "make good!"

Now, let's jump right into our next chapter, where we will identify how to ensure that your ads reach the right people, at the right time, to yield the desired results.

The Covert Code Mastering the Art of Digital Marketing The Covert Code Mastering the Art of Digital Marketing The Covert Code Mastering the Art of Digital Marketing The Covert Code Mastering the Art of Digital Marketing The Covert Code Mastering the Art of Digital Marketing The Covert Code Mastering the Art of Digital Marketing The Covert Code Mastering the Art of Digital Marketing The Covert Code Mastering the Art of Digital Marketing

01000011 01101
01101111 01100100 01100101 001000
001000
01101111 011001
01101111 01100100 011001
01101111 011001
01101111 01100110 00100000

CHAPTER SIX

RIGHT PEOPLE, RIGHT TIME, RIGHT RESPONSE

One of the biggest red flags for any business owner should be when your traditional media sales rep wants to sell you a digital solution that is outside of their own distribution. If your rep for NBC or Cox Radio wants to sell you streaming or display ads on their website, that's absolutely a good decision and will complement your traditional media campaign by extending your reach online. The price might not be competitive when compared to other digital tools to target your audience online, but you know what you are getting, and they know what they are selling. They should be able to prove to you that your digital ad or stream generated traffic to your website and how many views, watches, etc. were generated with G4 reporting. When you must sound the alarm is when that same rep tries to sell you online display targeting outside of their domain on the ad exchange. Why? Because they know nothing about online advertising. To stay relevant and continue to command a paycheck, they are reselling other digital media companies' products. The bottom line is that they have no control over the end product distribution and are not qualified to ask the right questions that protect their clients.

I first encountered this situation here in Oahu with a long-time client who purchased TV and radio directly (with the agency doing the digital, of course). During a status meeting, she shared with me several plans she had purchased to expand their online reach, and frankly, it sounded just too good to be true. When I probed deeper, it was obvious that none of the reps, or the powers that be, at any station could answer my questions about which publisher or CND they were engaging with to distribute ads through the ad exchange, how they identified the targeted audiences, or how they could verify that the impressions were delivered or that reported clicks were by humans versus bots.

The absolute clearest red flag is when they promote ad distribution using "geo-fencing," which involves targeting people who are in a specific geographic area in a much more targeted approach than simply by zip code. I'm talking about a football stadium, office building, housing community, even a military base. It sounds like a dream situation for a company that knows exactly who they want to reach, but the problem is that it doesn't work.

Typically, to target an individual online, you have two options. Their computer IP address is the easiest. The second is a user's device or cell phone/iPad, which does not have an IP but rather can be targeted via apps or chips. Most media companies will promise that they can match a user via fingerprint, that is, email matching. Assuming that the primary email is the same on a phone and computer, they lead us to believe that they can safely assume the user is the same and then serve ads to that individual over multiple devices using cross-device targeting. Until very recently, I still believed this was possible. Then I started to dig deeper and noticed that, unless I visited a website from my iPhone, I had never seen one of my own client's ads "cross-device." The plot thickens...

Most media companies who sell you on geo-fencing using display ads will say that they get a 95 percent fingerprint match on your phone and know the age range, gender, and location of the registered user. The problem is that the data is just too good to be true. There are too many different devices, permission settings, apps, and emails registered that are not "primary" (i.e., matching other devices, or can be legally collected and resold for marketing purposes). What if that user doesn't have a computer? Which other device are we matching with and how will they pixel tag that device? Your bullshit detector should be flashing. Honestly, even if we could match with 20 percent of the phones with certainty, that would still be enough to warrant a paid ad, depending on the cost for most companies, so why not be honest from the start? That brings us to our next problem.

Assuming we could target these attendees at a trade show, how many ads could we reasonably deliver to each person, and over what period? Well, that depends on which media publisher you engage to distribute your ads through the display network and how aggressive your bidding strategy is. Now ask yourself, if you are trying to reach attendees at a trade show, wouldn't it be essential to reach them while they are there, or at least within a reasonable amount of time after the show to stay top of mind? Do you think an average frequency of two ads over thirty days is going to break through the noise of everything else they're doing or seeing on their smartphone? The answer is it won't, and if a partner tells you that they can deliver the ads over a shorter period with a higher frequency, then you should ask them to prove it to you because it doesn't add up with the technology we have today. Unless you are using an app on the phone or beacons at the event, or working with a publisher who is in control of the Wi-Fi, it's bogus. Here's how I found out.

It was March of 2015, and I was working with Hawaii Pacific Health, but specifically focused on Kapi`olani Medical Center for Women & Children. We had recently rebuilt their Hapai app (*hapai* means pregnant in Hawaiian) and experienced success with search intent ads. The marketing director wanted to expand, and geo-fencing was on the tip of everyone's tongue. And it seemed fair enough, our hospitals were large geographically, and back then there were fewer security and privacy protocols in place on smartphones and most people didn't think twice about sharing location information or turning off apps that tracked location. So, we launched a campaign targeting women who visited the hospital with three different messaging strategies based on their age. For women eighteen to thirty-five, they would be served the Hapai pregnancy app, for thirty-six to fifty-five we served a keiki pediatrics ad (for children), and for women over fifty-six we would serve a mammogram ad. Our assumption was that, since the hospital also had doctors' offices, we would have a healthy population to target and hopefully cross-market different unique services to increase our brand recognition and loyalty. The campaign started, and impressions were served. At the time it was harder to track results because, except for downloading the Hapai app, our ads were focused on brand awareness and did not have a hard conversion. I was looking for CPM cost, click-through rates, un-bounced traffic increases, increased time spent on those featured services content sections on the website... soft metrics. But for the Hapai app, I did have the app download as a conversion goal. The issue was that we didn't have a way to track the source of traffic before the user got to the Apple Store or Google Play to download. If someone clicked from the ad to download, we couldn't give our ad credit necessarily because the transaction happened outside of our website on a third-party site. The Apple Store doesn't share website analytics with app publishers and UTMs don't work outside of your domain. We also had similar expectations from our media partner at the time that a campaign like this would take 90–120 days to really show measurable results because we needed enough users to create an audience pool and essentially get enough data to make meaningful conclusions on the campaign's success. How much is enough, you say? Well, that depends on the company size, industry, and what type of testing is being conducted. If it's A/B creative, then the answer may be never, as we will discuss more later, but regardless, each company must set some baseline that fairly represents their audience AND customer's journey.

So, the campaign launched, and pregnant women did start to download the app. From the first reports provided by the media company, everything looked great—strong click-through rates, valid un-bounced website traffic, low CPM impressions, etc. Time went by (we passed the sixty-day mark), but I didn't see any significant lift in the other campaign soft goals. Could it be that our creativity wasn't resonating? Could it be that those older women turned their phones off at night, and our cookies got removed as they only went to potentially one doctor's visit a year, and we just didn't have enough impressions per user? After a sleepless night, I decided to start with the easiest way to level the playing field. Instead of sending the Hapai ads directly to download the app, I created a landing page on our website with some light overview copy and links to both Apple and Google Play. Then, I added Google Analytics event goals to fire on each button click off-site (because URL destination goals in UA/G4 Analytics also don't work for sites outside of your domain) and then took it one step further and updated all of our ads with very specific UTM parameters for each creative set and ad size.

Next, I redeployed the campaign and waited. The reports provided by the media company basically looked the same as the previous period. Now that I had enhanced tracking, it was clear that something was fishy, because the data did not match Google Analytics. The reported clicks on the ads did not match up to users, even if I included bounced traffic. Not even close. So, I went to our partner with my new data and asked for an explanation. My poor rep didn't know what to say when I showed him all my data points. The best answer IT could provide was that users might have clicked on the ads twice or that the Google Analytics code wasn't placed correctly. Eventually, they came back and said that it had been a reporting malfunction on their end. For our campaign's final thirty days, to prove that the campaign was growing brand awareness to our audience pool, they promised to triple our impressions (estimated frequency per user 9× over thirty days). OK, great, I thought. But how do I know that these extra impressions are being delivered unless I see them for myself? So, I decided to create a personal focus group. Being a woman in her thirties with a child who was born at Kapiʻolani, I was the ideal target audience for my own campaign. I waited seven days to give the media partner the most time possible to rev up inventory and drove down to the hospital. I parked and took a forty-five-minute walk around the lobby, went up and down some elevators, and had a coffee at the cafeteria before walking back to my car. Then, I sat in the lot for fifteen minutes browsing popular sites from my iPhone like Yahoo, KHON2, KITV, Food Network, CNN, etc. I scrolled and scrolled. No Hapai ads. Perhaps, I thought, it took a while for the match to happen? I drove home and repeated the exercise, and over the next seven days, I spent fifteen minutes every day actively searching—iPhone, iPad, and on my computer. I saw plenty of ads, but not one from Kapiʻolani. Could I have been in the 5 percent of the unmatched fingerprint mapping pool? That's when I asked my media partner for a list of emails that they had collected to create this audience pool as proof, but as you might expect, that was not something that they were able to pull and no, they couldn't provide screenshots of the ads delivered through the network to match the report of delivered impressions or destination URLs either.

We ended the campaign, and two years later that company was no longer in business, but I did get a call from my old rep. He had moved to Quantcast, the leader in real-time behavior targeting, and was ecstatic to tell me about what he had learned. "Anna, you were right," he started. I stopped typing and sat up taller in my chair. "Turns out that last company and most *top-funnel* media companies are acquiring lists to target customers, and those are being sold and resold sometimes up to two years after the initial data was collected." I was floored. That's why those top-funnel media companies state that, for the campaign to become effective, it needs to run for 90+ days because chances are that customers are no longer looking for what you're selling. What does that mean? Essentially, to create a geo-fencing audience, the media company purchases lists of people. In this case, it was data from the "eBay Behavioral Audience" who match the criteria and live around the area. Then, they try to target that user through an email match and deliver an ad to them on a device. Think about it: Have you ever seen an ad from a retailer right after shopping there? Don't you think you should? Unless they have an app that is tracking your location and can match you with an online profile, it's just not possible. And that's the reason why all these big retailers and brands have apps. It's to allow them the ability to reach you *for real*.

 ANNA'S TIP

Ask your media partner how they acquire their data. If the answer is "lists" or if they use the word "geo-fencing," back away slowly.

Sadly most "top of the funnel" digital media companies use lists to target customers, which, as you have learned, is a gigantic red flag. Here's why: Let's say that my mother is going to a baby shower. She goes to eBay and purchases a stroller. This puts her on a list that says she's the parent of a toddler. Then that list is sold and resold to companies trying to target "parents of a toddler," who then try and locate her email online, reestablish a pixel, and deliver her a banner ad (impression). As you recall, our "matching" is poor at best. Even today, only about 40 percent of emails can be matched with an active IP address (and that's only possible with companies that have so many pixels placed that they have the power to play and enough saturation to make this connection), and soon, with the new privacy rules rolling out, selling personal information to a third party in this manner won't even be legal. The second and more critical problem is that my mother is not the parent of a toddler, so assuming the partner could find her online, it's just a total waste.

Quantcast, on the other hand, uses real-time behavior data to target the customer right at the moment of intent. This means that we know with certainty that this is our target audience and that they are in the market for whatever we are selling. Quantcast started off as a data company and provides incredible audience insights for your website traffic—which cars they drive, which shows they watch, what fast food they like, what other sites they visit, if they're business owners... I'm talking *deep*. How they learn this information is based on a *lot* of data. Through millions of partnerships, Quantcast has over 100+ million pixels that allow them to track behavior insights and develop patterns together with the power of AI, machine learning, and real-time data, making it simple to understand your customers today and predict your audiences of tomorrow. This is called first-party data, meaning it's collected by Quantcast through their own proprietary pixel, which is placed on partner sites.

Not only do we know that the person we are targeting is in-market for the product we are selling, but we can also reach them at the exact moment of intent. My mom typically reads on her iPad in the morning and visits the same ten sites in common with another shopper on our site, so we will serve her an ad on StarAdvertiser between 6:00 and 8:00 a.m. Unlike those "top of funnel" imposters, Quantcast would have known that my mother was not the parent of a toddler because, if she had been, she would have performed a plethora of other online searches and actions to prove it. A single stroller purchase would *never* have flagged her. Not only could they determine if you were in-market but also when you were out of the market because your pattern changed. For example, after reviewing a couple hundred solar company websites with Quantcast pixels placed, we learned that the average homeowner, depending on the size of the market and overall awareness of solar, would visit four to six sites during their research phase "intent." Then the lion's share of those users would select two to three companies to "request a free quote" between twenty-eight and thirty-two days later. Based on each user's journey, the algorithm is rebuilding its model in real time, and would be able to determine that this IP that showed interest in solar has now completed two competitor quotes and then stopped revisiting other solar sites they had previously visited, indicating that they are out of the market (done for now). Thus, we'll stop serving them ads immediately in real time. The process is the same with all types of products and services. We build a model, learn, keep learning, and then become more efficient, reducing the amount of media waste and overall consumer noise. I'm sure we have all felt irritated by ads that are just taking up space in your display. Quantcast knows this and adapts to your unique user behavior, but other front-funnel companies don't.

Sounds too good to be true? To make sure I wasn't being naïve, I asked for a delivery report and proof that my impressions ran, which they happily provided. OK, so why doesn't everyone use this magical tool? The answer is that they don't understand that awareness advertising online is not the same as intent advertising. It takes longer and is more expensive. The ROI is not easy to see right away. I learned that the hard way.

It was May of 2018, and I was working with one of my big solar companies in California when a new marketing director was hired. He was a believer in digital, and so we got along just swimmingly. I shared Quantcast with him, and he was chomping to make a big splash. "If we need to spend $100k a month, we will," he told me during one of our status calls. WOW, this guy was a baller, I thought, let's do this. We started a multilayered campaign—competitive conquesting, native ads, display, pre-roll, we had it all. Competitive conquesting has always been one of my favorite products. How it works is we provide a list of competitor URLs, and then Quantcast places a virtual "fence" around those domains. When visitors arrive, using real-time behavioral analysis, we can determine if they're in-market, tag them, and then serve them ads along their customer journey through the display network. This is possible because, although we don't have a tag on the competitor's site, we do have enough pixel saturation in the worldwide web and then can plot the traffic path, that is, the user went to CNN –> Competitor.com -> New York Magazine -> BOOM!

We launched the campaign with an aggressive budget, spending $70K over the first ninety days. I thought things were going great when I got a call from the owner. He was livid. The marketing director had been fired, and so we set up an emergency meeting. I called my rep, and we put together a deck showing all the results from our campaign. I didn't even get halfway through my presentation when he started screaming. "I'm happy you like your data, I want you to like your data, but on my side, the numbers are not lining up." He was right. All of the traffic and clicks didn't mean anything without users turning into leads. Not later, *now*. We killed the campaign and refocused all of our budget on lower funnel intent marketing, which was easy to attribute. Overall, the campaign had been a success, but it wasn't until six months later that we saw the lift and ended the year with the highest books reported in the company's history. Was it Quantcast? We will never know, but it doesn't seem to be a coincidence that more highly targeted website traffic = more online leads. And that's why now, before I start any campaign, I mandate that clients go through my digital media best practices presentation and that we "level set" on when they can expect their investment to be returned. Depending on the industry, time of year, and competitiveness, most B2C businesses, except for retail, see thirty to ninety days from the first visit to sale from intent marketing. For awareness and consideration funnel campaigns, unless you're willing to commit to six months at a minimum, it's considered bad decision-making. As a result, my agency typically achieves client goals with search intent marketing and other lower funnel media tools. This has begun to shift recently. We're noticing that online behavior is changing and our clients are getting "tapped out," meaning that through optimization we are not able to get more search clicks on our paid campaigns on Google or Microsoft exchanges. There are only so many people in our desired geographic areas searching for products and solutions, and we want to expand reach and get more leads at a low cost-per-acquisition, but how? That's how I was introduced to programmatic advertising.

PROGRAMMATIC ADVERTISING

Today, luckily, there are other options to reach the right person at the right moment quickly and for a fraction of the cost. The problem with Quantcast was that it required a minimum spend and was controlled by the media company versus self-served (meaning that someone like myself could manage my own campaigns, set bids, control targeting, etc.). Just like the barrier of entry that exists with traditional advertising, these requirements limit the ability of smaller or medium-sized businesses to engage, as they require large investments in money and time. For example, if you want to sponsor a billboard, you have to pay for the installation and then are required to keep the ad running for at least three months (and if you want to change the ad creative at any time during your contract, you're required to pay for the printing and installation). The same is true with radio or other forms of traditional media. You have some control but not much; you can't pick exactly what time your spot airs or which page your ad is placed on (you can try, but it's not guaranteed). The benefits of programmatic advertising are that finally advertisers of all sizes can target users digitally and along all stages of the full purchase funnel without any long-term commitment and with messaging that is tailored and targeted. Before we dive deeper, let's circle back to the concept of the customer journey, but this time as it applies to advertising.

As you recall, the customer must see and experience our brand multiple times before moving from Awareness to Action (buying something or arriving at the website). So, our job as marketers is to figure out how many times a day we can insert ourselves into our target audience's radar to build audience share of mind.

Here's an example: Bob lives in San Francisco and works downtown. He uses a cell phone alarm, and once it goes off, he likes to lay in bed for ten minutes to fully wake up, scrolling through posts on Facebook and the CNN news feed. Then he gets up and turns on the morning news while he makes coffee and eats yogurt. It's time to go to work, and he puts on his earbuds, queues up Spotify, and walks a few blocks to catch the trolley to work. While on the trolley, he gazes out the window. Finally, when he's close to the office, he opens his Gmail and starts to read work-related messages.

How many media types does our brand have to reach Bob on his journey to work? As we can see, even before Bob gets to his desk, there were a plethora of opportunities for us to insert ourselves and gain impression share:

- Facebook ads, display, native, or video ads on CNN News (in bed)
- TV sponsorship/ads (during breakfast)
- Programmatic radio/streaming (on the way to the trolley)
- Programmatic out-of-home or traditional billboards/outdoor media/trolley ads (on the ride)
- Email marketing (Gmail)

This extra layer of the customer journey is key when building your media plan and website click paths because, before you start any paid advertising, you will need to determine how you will track results from each initiative and how to create the right content and landing page to support it.

Back to programmatic advertising: my preferred partner is StackAdapt, which is an open DSP or ad buying platform that allows advertisers to purchase digital ad inventory over multiple platforms and touchpoints with targeting tactics like venue type and geo radius, which can also help advertisers reach customers when they are in the right state of mind, increasing the opportunity to move them from consideration to purchase. The StackAdapt inventory allows for digital delivery across display, native, video, CTV, audio, in-game, and DOOH and allows for incredible forecasting options that help advertisers plan budgets and set expectations for spend and results.

TARGETING ON STEROIDS

There are two key ways to target your desired audience. Those boil down to first-party and third-party data sources. First-party data is primarily your data. The most common ways to obtain this data include placing a pixel on your website and tracking user traffic, or by using your CRM data, which creates a seed population of users (assuming we can match them). Quantcast, as we have mentioned, offers advertisers access to their proprietary first-party data as they have over 100+ million pixels measuring user behavior, allowing you to reach the desired audience at the moment of intent, at scale. Third-party data is inventory from data partners that provide reach to users they have collected across the ad exchange or through various methods. StackAdapt offers advertisers real-time instant access to multiple inventory partners as well as the ability to request more unique data sets in a couple of days.

 ANNA'S TIP

Make sure to ask how your partner acquires data and that when using third-party sources how they created those seed lists. This includes the age of the data, that is, thirty-day refreshed list of Individuals who are New Homeowners based on surveys, social media data, sweepstakes, online activity, public records, and purchase data.

Let's go through an example of the steps to create a campaign in StackAdapt.[7] If our company was looking for people interested in purchasing a new car, we could go to the audience tab/third-party segments and then type in car owners. The results populate, and now I can see the inventory source, how the data was acquired (segment description), audience size, and the average bid CPM to reach users by media type. Once I have selected my audiences, to determine my potential reach and drill down deeper into audience interests, I can use the forecasting tool.

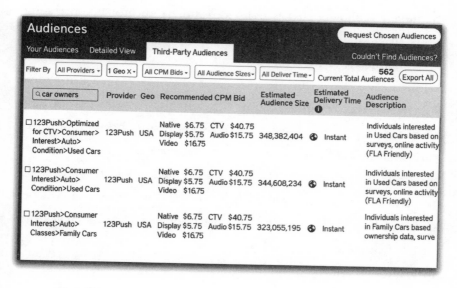

In the "planning" tab, we select forecasting and set our location to "Denver Colorado" before proceeding to the audience builder to set demographics (ages 18–54), interests (new or used car buyers), and those third-party audience lists. Next, we select the types of media we wish to use. In this case, I will select display and native, as they do not require any additional expense, that is, hiring a voice talent or creating a video asset. StackAdapt also allows advertisers to drill down

---

7   Go to thecovertcode.com/resources to watch me build a campaign.

further into the inventory (third-party data providers), but as this is our first campaign, we don't know enough yet about the quality of one third-party data source over another and thus will not exclude or narrow our forecast. We will set a lifetime for our campaign of thirty days and set budgets at $2k per media type and bid, taking into consideration the estimates we saw on the audience inventory tab for CPMs: Display $5.75, Native $6.50. Now the forecast comes back with insightful results. Our campaign is set to reach 30,778 people with twenty-one messages over thirty days. Although a per-day frequency is shown, that is not a very pure indicator because some users are online more than others, so it's more of an average. That's OK, the metric to look for is overall frequency and "overlap among selected channels," which indicates our likelihood to reach the same user over selected channels during the campaign. So now that we have some baseline of spend, we can make some assumptions on how this campaign will influence website traffic and user action. If we take the total number of estimated clicks (5,517), that would mean that a 1 percent conversion rate would generate fifty-five leads at a cost per click of $108.75. That is more than we budgeted, right? Well yes, but that benchmark was taken from all traffic generated and untargeted messaging. If critical mass messaging can yield a 2 percent conversion rate, then it's fair to expect we can generate the same (if not more) from targeted digital, assuming our ad creative and landing page are compelling. A 2 percent conversion would then bring our total leads to 110 at a cost per click of $54, which is better (in line with last year's budget and results), but still higher than our target. The next step is to determine how much we need in the lower funnel to support sales goals—search marketing budget as well as a healthy remarketing budget to ensure those new site visitors we drove from the top of the funnel are fully engaged (seeing enough impressions/frequency to move them through the purchase funnel) and have the highest likelihood of completing the "schedule appointment" or purchasing over the historical conversion time.

To conclude this chapter, remember that, even with these new tools at our disposal, they are still focused primarily on customers at the top of the funnel. Companies should only engage once they fully understand how to maximize potential at the lower funnel, which is easier to track and faster to convert. Lastly, with the industry shifting toward the cookieless future, it's even more important to partner with companies as mentioned previously to continue to serve ads to users online. To learn more about the cookieless future visit our resource section.

Code Ma
ring th
rt of D
tal Mar
ing Thi
ert Cod
asterin
he Art
Digital
rketing
 Art of
 Art of
de Art
ng the
 of Dig
l Marke
gThe Co
t Code
tering
 Art of
ring th
rt of D
tal Mar
ing Thi
ert Cod
asterin
he Art
Digital
rketing
 Covert
 Art Co
de Art
ng the
 of Dig
l Marke
gThe Co
t Code
tering
 Covert
de Code
tering
gThe Co
t Code
tering

01000011 01101
01101111 01100100 01100101 00100
00100
01101111 01100
01101111 01100100 01100
01101111 01100
01101111 01100110 00100000

CHAPTER SEVEN

SEARCH MARKETING DECODED

Moving right down the funnel, the next topic covers "intent," which breaks into two parts: search optimization (SEO, which is organic search traffic, i.e., earned) and SEM, which is paid and split among Google Ads (approximately 80 percent of search) and Microsoft Ads (20 percent of search, including Bing, Yahoo, and AOL). A search engine's job is to deliver the best content to the consumer. How search engines make money is by having high user adoption, so the goal of Chrome, Firefox, Safari, Edge, DuckDuckGo, and all of the search engines is to command more searches from their browsers and become the default browser on every device you own. The more daily users they maintain, the easier it is to monetize this access and sell their influence to advertisers and political powers. For them to gain loyalty (adoption), they need to create the best browsing experience possible. That means delivering the best, most relevant content to the consumer so they can find what they're looking for fast, very fast (on the first page of results). It also means providing a safe, secure place to browse and enjoy content and communities across devices seamlessly—the fewer interruptions, the better. It's a business.

Let's break it down starting with SEO, but as this book is focused on digital marketing, we're going to just touch lightly on SEO and then you can read the full saga on the resource section at *thecovertcode.com*.

SEARCH ENGINE OPTIMIZATION (SEO)

To this day, SEO is one of the most common things clients ask about. Is it worth spending money on? This topic is sure to upset a lot of people, but believe me when I tell you that committing to paid SEO services is one of the easiest ways to be taken advantage of as a business owner. In my opinion, it is the darkest of the dark digital art and I have seen too many business owners make the mistake of committing to paid SEO services by picking providers that don't provide the correct reporting or long-tail strategies that lift and hold rank.

SEO breaks into two sections, on-site and off-site, and like all digital tools, has changed dramatically over the past few decades.

ON-SITE SEO

As we've learned, it's critical that companies have a well-defined content strategy on their website. Once a site is launched and "turned on" to search engines, the next thing that a business must do is to submit your sitemap to Google Search Console, Bing, and other engines (optional). That then tells them that you exist and, after some time, they will deploy tiny little robots to go out and scan your website content to determine how valuable your site is with regard to the rest of the worldwide web. This includes crawling (text, images, and videos for keyword data collection), but the most important thing to remember is that a robot can't read an image, so if we want that content to "count," we need to provide a written description of the image or video, so that the search engine can add those keywords to our total score or rank. We call these alt tags, and they go behind the picture in code, but are shown over the image to the end user when you hover (optional but recommended). Alt tags are also being used by disabled people and are an important part of website accessibility. For example, a computer reader could describe the visuals on your site, such as a scenic picture of Diamond Head with a rainbow over Waikiki showcasing the beach, condos, and the famous Royal Hawaiian Hotel. Alt tags should also be used to identify button actions, since not all website users have the same visual abilities: "This is a button that takes you to a free quote page." In fact, approximately 20 percent of all website users[8] are now classified as disabled in some way, including being legally blind, color-blind, or limbless.

In addition to clear alt tags, each page/post of website content should contain a Meta Title, Meta Description, and Meta Keyword so when your company's listing is displayed in search, it's clear to the customer who you are and what they can expect to see after clicking through to your website.

---

8   "Accessibility fundamentals overview," Web Accessibility Initiative, updated August 8, 2023, https://www.w3.org/WAI/fundamentals/; "33 Accessibility statistics you need to know in 2023," monsido, November 16, 2022, https://monsido.com/blog/accessibility-statistics.

ANNA'S TIP

Make your alt tags as descriptive as possible, which will increase the total keywords on your site and ensure that all users will have the best experience. To make on-page SEO easier, install a plug-in like Yoast (WordPress) that will help you write meta titles that are the correct length. Visit *thecovertcode.com* for detailed tips on on-site SEO.

OFF-SITE SEO

This strategy is focused on getting articles and links that reference your brand and company URL posted on other reputable domains. Reputable means that they command over 10,000 unique daily visits. These strategies are called backlink building, and help search engines identify that one website is more valuable to the customer searching than another, because there are 50+ references to them over the web. There are several methods to build off-site links, some very time-consuming, but I've found that the best way to build credible backlinks at the lowest cost (time and money) is by submitting a company press release through a distribution service like EINnewsire.com. For a very low distribution cost, your controlled content is picked up by hundreds of news and other high-ranked sites, all containing those valuable links back to your site, building your off-site rank. Social media is also considered an off-site SEO tool; we'll talk more about it in chapter 9.

If you are a company paying for off-site SEO services, note that every month you should be presented with a current report of your site's rank based on a list of keyword phrases. You should be provided two reports, one for the full universe of Google and one that is localized (i.e., what would someone searching in Seattle potentially see). Your SEO partner should also be telling you when they expect to lift your rank from its current position to a future desired page 1 position of 1–10, which is the maximum number of organic listings per page on search engines. And then, you also should have a list of keyword phrases that you are watching and working on moving in rank or index.

You should also be receiving proof (links) to the published articles on whatever distribution channel they are using, as well as reports on how many references to your off-site content have been published. For companies that are just getting started, don't even engage in these paid SEO services unless you are willing to commit for two to three years and are happy not to receive any measurable ROI. The better solution is to use paid ads, which can guarantee results!

SEARCH ENGINE MARKETING (SEM)

When I started my first campaign on Google Ads, it was called AdWords. I had just launched my first WordPress website for Harris Therapy in 2011 and was feeling pumped. The focus of our campaigns was to promote physical therapy, occupational therapy, and speech therapy services and it seemed pretty straightforward. I clicked through the quick start setup and added a credit card. Not even a day had passed when I got a call from my Google rep. I was thrilled. I asked questions and basically just did as I was told, adding site link extensions, more headlines, additional keyword types, etc. And it worked. Well, at least I thought so at the time. It continued like this for the next two years; every six months, a new rep would call and tell me they were going to "optimize" my account. It wasn't until the fourth rep that I started to question the system. "But we just removed the phrase match keywords, why would we be adding them back in?" I asked and they told me some reason. As a novice, I again did what I was told. They were Google and wanted to help me make the most out of my campaign, right? *I trusted them...*

It wasn't until several years later, when I started my own agency and had multiple accounts that I began to question their recommendations. During one of my routine calls with Google, I finally had the sense that I was speaking with someone knowledgeable. His name was Chris, and he was stationed in Chicago. We instantly jived. By then, I had a lot of questions to ask and unlike any rep of the past, he wasn't just reading a script. Over the next year, I was able to switch most of my accounts over to him, which was very rare. We spoke regularly, and together, learned even more about the platform.

ANNA'S TIP

To this day, Google will not allow clients or agencies to stay with the same rep. The only exception is if you are an agency-approved Google advertiser, but that requires you to manage all accounts from a single account, which is not ideal because you can't separate billing (i.e., use different payment methods). This also influences your ability to report on clients' measured conversions because the full account will link to all of their G4 accounts. The overall result is not favorable for anyone. For business owners reading this, you now have no control of your account to verify that your ads ran or conversions fired. Best practice is to set up your own verified business account and then grant third-party access to your agency or team to manage on your behalf, always maintaining ownership level and billing control.

After some time, Chris was removed from my account, but by then I had mastered the platform. Once I knew basic concepts, I was able to play the game. When AdWords rebranded to Google Ads and changed the settings in July of 2018, it was easy for us to pivot, unlike so many other companies who set and forgot campaign strategies or failed to opt out of Google automatic changes.

STARTING YOUR FIRST CAMPAIGN

During your initial Google Ads campaign creation, you will be forced into a "Smart Campaign" setup. Just skip whatever isn't mandated so you can get to the end as fast as possible because you never ever want to let Google control anything about your account. Once you get into your account dashboard, you will go straight to the campaign and pause it. Next, click on the Settings icon in the top right corner and then select Switch to Expert Mode. You will also need to make sure to verify your company identity or risk the account being suspended (it's happening more frequently). The reasons for your account being suspended usually relate to the credit card on file not matching with the authorized user, or a business signing up with a Yahoo.com, AOL.com, or some other personal email that does not match their company domain, potentially flagging them as risky. There have been several times that, even with a company email, clients' accounts were suspended and it was impossible to get Google to remove the hold (on average three to five weeks of multiple calls, emails, and client heartache). For this reason, I recommend that as soon as you set up your account, go straight to verification and complete the process. The verification process will ask you to submit proof of your company ownership by uploading an EIN (.pdf) or other documents, as well as pictures of the front and back of a valid driver's license.

On the positive note, verification was implemented to protect both businesses and consumers, and emerged from the growing number of online scammers who were creating fake business websites that looked like the real deal and then used paid search to fool customers into believing that they were that said retailer. They'd run for a couple of weeks, taking customer orders, and then shut everything down and start over, leaving customers burned and the legit business out of a sale and with damaging and undeserved negative reviews.

Once you pause your Smart Campaign, it's time to build your first Expert campaign. Start by clicking "view all campaigns" and then select "search campaigns" and then click the + Create button and select Campaign. Next, you'll want to pick an objective. For most advertisers, the best way to start is with "Website Traffic" because we want to set a baseline and to do that we need as many clicks as possible to feed your website and establish your first visit to conversion rate. Only if you are trying to drive foot traffic to your shop would you change this and select "local store visits and promotions," but then you must ask yourself if Google Search is the best option based on your objectives and goals. Nextdoor or featured Yelp ads might be a better choice to drive foot traffic to your store.

Download your own campaign setup cheat sheet at thecovert-code.com

My recommendation is to always start with a focus of generating qualified website traffic, and after we establish a baseline can adjust to focus on "sales" to see if we can lift impression share and overall results (optimization strategy). In your campaign settings, there are several primary factors that will make or break your online success: Networks, Locations, Budgets, Bidding, and Keywords. For those with existing campaigns, to change settings go to each campaign (not ad group) and edit active campaigns.

WHEN NETWORKING IS NOT GOOD FOR BUSINESS

There are three options to distribute ads on Google but only one that is 100 percent controlled by Google: "Google Search Network." The default setting when you create a new campaign will include all three—"Google Search Network, Search Partners, Display Network"—so the first step is to uncheck Search Network and Display Network and then push save.

The "search partners" is essentially the same as the "display network," meaning that your ads are running on inventory *outside* of Google.com. The only difference is the type of ad creative. Search are text ads. Display are image or video ads. Regardless of the ad type, all that matters to us is that they are served outside of Google on a third-party website or app. Remember how the ad exchange works: every impression shown to a visitor on company.com is paid by the publisher to the site owner. For example, if you visit covertcommunication.com and leave, you will see remarketing ads that are being served to you on the display network from Criteo. As you browse online to your favorite sites, every ad impression shown to you is being paid by Criteo to that domain.

That means that if you select those network options, Google must pay their partner each time they serve your ad. But how does Google get paid? It's based on a CPC model. Aha! It is for that very reason they made that radical change to bid strategies a couple of years ago, which reduced the options for advertisers from eight unique strategies to just three. Google was simply not making enough money, and with the growth of media publishing competitors, they were no longer the only game in town, but they were still acting like they were. Think about it: How many impressions did the 100-pound gorilla have to serve outside of Google to generate one click? Maybe that click's bid was just $0.50 or less and had a low click-through rate. That meant that they were paying partners more than what they were billing customers, which was not great math for Google. So, they tipped the cards in their favor by changing the bidding strategies and, you guessed it, employing bots to click on ads to make sure they got paid enough to pay partners.

Now, you must ask yourself the question: Did they even serve my impression? I have countless memories of clients who came to the agency and said, "We do remarketing with Google." My reply was typically this: "I've been to your site and haven't seen any ads yet, but that might be due to my location. Have you ever seen your own ad?" Silence, followed by a "maybe," or "no, we haven't," to which I reply, "How do you know it ever ran?" Recently, when I was doing some consulting for a large SunPower dealer, the marketing manager said, "I think the pixel wasn't set up correctly or something because the numbers seem off." I explained that there was no pixel for remarketing inside of Google and that it is controlled from G4 Analytics permissions that link website audiences to a Google Ads account. After logging in, we confirmed that those settings were active, so then why wasn't the data adding up? Because we have no way to verify if the reported impression ever ran.

Bottom line: you *only* ever want to advertise on the Google Search Network because that doesn't cost Google anything but the opportunity cost. They keep all the money and don't have to share a penny with partners. Their goal then becomes to see who is willing to pay the most out of all the advertisers who are bidding on those same keywords in that same geolocation. Then they show those ads more frequently and higher on the page to gobble up as much of the daily budget as possible. Makes sense, right? Now go ahead and take a moment to update your campaigns, and then let's get into bid strategies and budgets to see how we will use our new learning to increase our results at a decreased cost.

 ANNA'S TIP

Only use Google Search or Microsoft Search for intent ad campaigns. Do not use partners, display, or remarketing campaigns. The same rules apply on both platforms.

LOCATION, LOCATION, LOCATION!

In your "campaign settings," you have the option to set your geographic locations to target. The options include all countries and territories, United States and Canada, United States, or Enter Another Location. You always want to pick "enter another location" because even if you want to target all people living in the United States, the better way to build the campaign would be to add each state independently, so you can have visibility on your market penetration by state, and then can have more granular control over bids and the cost-per-conversion by market. The absolute best way to build a campaign is based on zip codes, which will give you valuable information on potential income levels, housing, and zoning. Then you can adjust your bids based on what you are willing to pay for a lead from that specific resident, by geography, to increase conversion rates and meet your company's goals.

Now it is important to mention that, a few years ago, some states enforced rules about targeting by postal code. Arizona, California, and several other states required that campaigns that mentioned rates, or financing terms, had a limited reach. Why? Well, some companies were using zip code targeting locations with financial messaging like "get quick cash now" schemes that had high interest rates and unethical terms to target low-income residents. The same is true with medically focused keywords. To protect the consumer, Google Ads limited the ability to serve these types of content messages by zip code, making it harder to reach and more expensive for the advertiser. Sure, the concept seems fair, but what I have found is that more AI technology or manual oversight is required to make this work as intended, because many of our clients do not violate the policy but are still flagged. For example, most solar companies offer "zero down-financing" with no strings attached. You pay less than your current utility bill and the payments to the new solar loan provider don't start until your system is on, saving money and the world. Similarly, we have a client, Total Image Hair & Wig Restoration Center in LA, who creates "real human hair medical wigs" for cancer patients and those suffering from lupus and other medical conditions. They aren't giving medical advice. Flags can be placed on all types of campaigns, including real estate, trade schools, consumer goods, etc. If your account is flagged, you can submit an appeal to Google and sometimes they will remove the limited reach, but not all of the time. This also applies to YouTube ads, which can be even more challenging to get violations removed.

COVERT CODE RULES FOR LOCATIONS

Start as granular as you can. If you have a storefront, always use a radius target for your office location so you have the potential to show in a Google Map Ad.

Click "Advanced Search" to add bulk locations and always double-check results. Often US zip codes will also match those in countries like France or Germany and you will need to exclude them. Sometimes, zip codes are not found at all. In this case, you can search for a city/county nearby or use the tool "nearby" in Google Map to find those locations that are not highlighted in your preview map.

If you launch a campaign and see that your ads are being limited, depending on the reason, start with an appeal and if that doesn't work, rebuild the campaigns using "city & counties" from the Advanced Search window. If that doesn't work, try to change your ad copy, removing the identified terms of concern, and submit a new appeal.

If you truly do want to reach all fifty states, ask yourself some hard questions. Where is our best product/service saturation? Where do we want to grow more? Where have we never really been able to make an impact? Then create three lists (best, middle, low) and three campaigns with those states targeted within each, so you can control your costs and make bid adjustments in the future (this means you can decide to increase or decrease over your set max CPC to be more effective). This will allow you to meet your campaign objectives from the "best" while learning about your other "middle" and "lower" audiences. Are search trends the same? Do our ad copy and landing page resonate with these audiences? Start small. The objective is to meet your company's KPI goals, and as seasonality and competitiveness change quickly, you want to be able to rapidly assess what is working and adjust so you don't overspend or underperform.

Anyone reading this chapter right now who manages a Google Ads campaign, stop what you're doing and log in. Go to campaigns, settings, locations, and then right under the options you will see a drop-down arrow with "location options." Click it and change from the default "presence or interest: People in, regularly in, or who've shown interest in your target locations (recommended)" option to the second "Presence: people in or regularly in your target locations." Scroll to the bottom and click save.

∧ Location options

Target ⑦

○ Presence or interest: People in, regularly in, or who've shown interest in your targeted
   locations (recommended)
◉ Presence: People in or regularly in your targeted locations

Cancel   Save

Why was this so important? I'll give you an example: Let's say that I'm selling roofing services in Oahu and create a campaign targeted at people living on the North Shore. Joe Doe in Texas is planning a family vacation to Hawaii for Christmas and is online searching for hotels, activities, and flights. In terms of Google search, he has "shown interest in our target recommendation."

Flash forward: a storm hits Houston, and his roof is leaking. He goes to Google and searches "roofing repair" or "best roofing company." Had we gone with Google's recommendation, our company's roofing ad would be served to this man in Texas because he has interest in Hawaii. The ad gets served, he clicks, gets to the website and then realizes that the roofer is in Oahu, and clicks right out. In fact, this is one of the single easiest ways to overspend or negatively impact your campaign results.

BUDGET: DANGLE THE CARROT

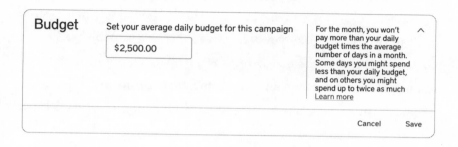

One of the biggest mistakes a company can make is setting a small daily campaign budget out of fear of overspending—$5 per day, $25 per day, etc. The problem with that is that you are guaranteeing that Google will spend all your funds quickly, and then your ad will not show for the rest of the day. This happened years ago when I started working with a big real estate investment company with a corporate office in New York. Every morning, the executives were up early, congratulating themselves on their high ad positioning. The problem was they had the wrong location settings (recommended versus physically located in) and other New Yorkers were also searching for real estate. With a low daily budget of just $50 and an average CPC of $7, it didn't take long for the budget to be fully spent (to the wrong people), and by the time residents in California got online (did I mention that Californians were the desired target audience?), the ads had already stopped showing. I'm bringing this up because you must make sure your location settings are correct before you use the budget rule I'm about to share with you or *you will overspend.*

The goal is to make sure that your ad has the greatest potential to show to people physically located in the area you care about, who are searching online for the exact services you offer. The metric that tells us this is called "search impression share" and our mission is for this percentage to be as high as possible because you only pay when someone clicks, not views, your ad. Think about your paid search goals in two pieces: brand awareness and increase valuable traffic. We want our ad to show as many times as possible in Google to reinforce our brand (views are free) and then generate high-quality visits (paid) while still protecting our budget by only allowing for one click per human (ClickCease) over a set period of time.

Let's look at another example of why we never want to set a low budget or let Google bid on our behalf. Let's say that you're selling [organic strawberries] in Los Angeles, and the average CPC is $2. If you set your daily budget at $10, then after you generate five clicks, what happens? Your ads stop showing. Or what if the average CPC is $11, then will your ad ever show? If you couple that by letting Google bid for you, let's say you have a very specific exact match key phrase that has low search share like [white albino strawberries], and since it's very niche and low competition, the average CPC is just $1. Google can, and will, spend all of your $10 daily budget on just one click. In fact, Google can spend 20 percent more per day (so $12), as long as they don't overspend over thirty days ($300).

ANNA'S TIP

Be careful when planning budgets in Google because they are based on thirty days from the start of your campaign, not monthly. This can impact your marketing reporting and also get you into trouble if you stop the campaign early, as they may have already spent more than they should (front-loaded) and you potentially could be missing out on impression share, that is, they have to continue to show your ad even if they overspend your budget. Always note your campaign date start and plan spend over the next thirty days for reporting.

It's for these reasons that you always want to set an aggressively high daily budget because you don't ever want to miss the opportunity to serve an ad to someone physically located in your geography, who is searching for a specific exact match keyword phrase, due to budget restrictions.

ANNA'S TIP

Don't panic and make rash decisions based on your optimization score or warning message from Google to switch your strategy. Every day, Google will make optimization recommendations on your account (the same ones every day). You just need to reject them and your score will go back up to 100 percent.

Let's get back to the budget and how it works with bidding and search impression share. What's important to remember is that there are eight possible ad positions on each page of Google Search Results: four at the top above organic search and four at the bottom (on every page). Sometimes even more if you count map ads or shopping ads; it all depends on the keywords being searched. This means that, as long as you are only advertising on the Google Search Network, you can have every confidence that your ads will show because Google has lots of inventory and wants customers to click. Our job is to make sure that the algorithm serves as many of those potential ad spaces with your brand as possible, 24/7.

To recap, we set a massive daily budget and dangle a carrot to the platform. "Hey Google, look at all this money we are willing to spend today! Do you want it? Come and try your best!" The result: you will have the opportunity to serve ads all day long and maximize impression share. Google still only gets paid when someone clicks, but they don't lose any money when someone doesn't. It's a win-win.

I know that many of you must be thinking, hell no, I'm scared to put a big daily budget on my account. But don't worry, that's when we protect ourselves using the correct bid strategy, which is one that *we control, not Google.* Under Bidding, change the recommended strategy from "conversions" to "clicks" and then set a maximum CPC limit.

Bidding	What do you want to focus on? ⑦	⌃
	Clicks ▾	
	Conversions is recommended for your campaign	
	☑ Set a maximum cost per click bid limit	
	Maximum CPC bid limit ⑦	
	$ 5.00	
	⚠ You've chosen to focus on **clicks** using the **Maximize clicks** bid strategy, but your account tracks conversions. You could get more conversions by choosing to focus on conversions	
	Or, select a bid strategy directly (not recommended)	

What is the absolute maximum that you are willing to spend on a person physically located in a geography you care about, searching exactly for your services? Of course, your bid might not be enough to get you a high impression share (50 percent or more) based on the competitiveness of your marketplace, time of year, or type of service, but at the very least you will be in control of your costs and learning market trends. Set your bid strategy to "maximum clicks" and add a comfortable amount. I usually start with $3–$5, regardless of industry and range, based on the total client's need for speed and my keyword planning forecast (we will get to that), and check the box "set a maximum cost per click bid limit," indicating to Google that you are not willing to spend a cent over that CPC. That doesn't mean that they will charge you that amount; it's the absolute most they can charge you. Often, our clients are spending much lower than our max bid, and that number gets better (cheaper) the longer we run campaigns and build online rank from organic on-site and off-site SEO efforts.

Now that you have controlled the maximum bid and made yourself very attractive to Google, all that you must do is watch your "Search Impression Share" and then, depending on your results, increase or decrease your max CPC by a few dollars at a time. Typically, I like to shoot for a 50 percent+ impression share from each campaign, but this can vary by industry. Bottom line: it's all about your goals and what a click and conversion are worth to you. If you are only showing to 10 percent of your desired audience, that's perfectly fine, as long as it is the right 10 percent and you are meeting your business goals for leads at the desired cost-per. Here are a few examples over the same time period to give you an idea.

Real Estate Company

Impression share	Conversions	Avg. CPC	Cost
< 10%	23.00	$0.54	$1.51K

Trade School

Search impr. share ▾	Conversions ▾	Avg. CPC ▾	Cost ▾
66.00%	113.00	$3.50	$8.03K

The more impression share you command, the more you will spend, because you have a greater chance of a customer clicking on your ad. I recommend that, once you set your initial campaign goals, start with the CPC that is in the middle of your forecast or around $3–$5. Then wait five to seven days for the initial learning to set and look at your campaign's impression share and your conversions by campaign. If you want more results, increase your max CPC bid by $1–$3 to start (depending on how far from 50 percent you are). If you are not getting the right results or have a high impression share (over 50 percent) and are way over your competitors (you can see this on the graph on the campaigns tab overview), then reduce your bid. Then repeat the process, checking campaigns regularly as bids can swing dramatically day by day because of other factors out of your control. Big companies often do what I call "Sweeps," where they will allocate hundreds of thousands to penetrate a market or run a promotion. They buy the media in mass, just like TV, and are after one thing: impression share to help their other advertising efforts and support a product launch or promotion. The good news is that these big budgets and initiatives don't last long. For instance, you might have seen that a $7 CPC bid for your HVAC campaign had a 45 percent impression share over the past six weeks without much change. Suddenly, it's down to >10 percent. You could increase to $15 and try and compete with whatever competition just came online, or you could wait a week and usually it will flatten back out. You could also check your campaign's locations report to see if ads serving in a specific region, state, or zip code are responsible for the overall drop and make a manual adjustment to increase bids for those unique locations (i.e., add a 50 percent bid adjustment for users located in Orlando). You need to keep watch and always think about seasonality and other environmental effects that could be influencing your campaign.

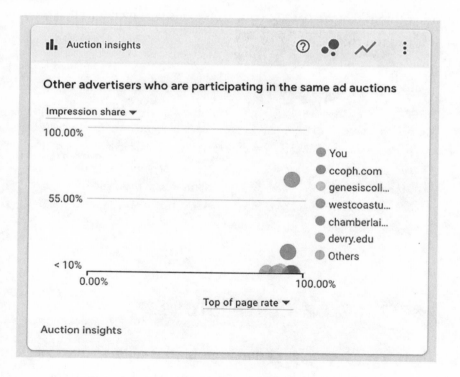

You might be asking yourself, *how do the other bid strategies work?* My recommendation is to simply know that they are all controlled by Google and based on delivering "conversions," which sounds great in concept, but the problem is that just because a conversion is reported in Google does not mean that click turned into a sale for your business. Unless you have a retail store and a full transaction is being collected, the conversion is just a lead. And it might not even be a lead. For example, a common conversion goal for Google to report on is "calls that last over sixty seconds," but that doesn't mean the person who called was a new customer or booked an appointment. They might have been an existing customer, a solicitor, a partner.... It's not Google's fault, they can't know the full picture unless they have more data, and it is possible to set up Salesforce or other integrations to help close the gap, but then you must rely on sales processes and other things that are hard to control as a business owner or marketer. It is just too risky.

 ANNA'S TIP

Always use CallTracking and listen to calls generated from your paid search campaigns, manually tagging them as a qualified lead or, if not, add clear tags like solicitor, service not provided, out of territory, or wrong company, so you can identify patterns in search and drill down to your true cost-per-lead by campaign and paid source.

SETTING UP CONVERSIONS

The next step is to import your G4 goals (hard and soft) into Google Ads and then set the hard ones as primary and soft as secondary. "Primary conversions" will all count on your Google Ads dashboard by campaign, and secondary actions will track (log for each) but not be part of your "cost-per-conversion" total on the rollup (the screen where you see your search impression share and overall insights data). You should always make your "hard conversions" primary goals and "soft conversions" secondary goals. This way you can drill down closer to what your true cost-per-lead and cost-per-sale are from your Google campaigns. Since first-time visitors are one of our most important metrics to back out our estimated budgets, I recommend including that into primary conversions for the simple reason that you want to increase website traffic and get enough unique visits to your new website so that you will have enough data to make future predictions on traffic conversion rates by paid SEM source. Remember, the search engine's job is to provide the best, most relevant results for users. Google knows this (or thinks they know) from tracking conversions generated by a user clicking on a paid ad and arriving at your website. If Google can't "take credit" and show their value, then it will start to view your website as the problem, that is, all these customers clicked on this ad and only 1 percent converted? Something must be wrong with the landing page, so let's show a competitor's ad and decrease the amount of times we show this ad. By allowing first_visit to be included as a primary conversion, you will fool the algorithm into serving your ad more often, resulting in a lower overall CPC and higher impression share long term. Then you will just use the tools you already learned to login into G4 and determine out of all the paid Google traffic how many leads (or hard conversions) you actually got.

ANNA'S TIP

There are ways to view the number of conversions at a granular level inside of Google, which can help you get an idea of how well you're doing without leaving the platform. Just click "tools and settings" under measurement "conversions" in the top left corner, select "view all conversion actions," and now you can see each, and the total count as well as repeat rate (same customer fired two events).

Now that you have your campaign settings all set up for success, the next most important thing is your keyword strategy and to make sure you are in full control of when your ad has the opportunity to be served.

Today in Google there are three types of keywords: exact match, phrase match, and broad match. Exact match is the safest because then you will have more control over when your ad shows. I say "more" because, even with your exact match keywords, Google doesn't always stay true to your campaign settings. They take liberties and will slide in other search terms (close variations) that favor more impression share. For example, it's common that if you put an exact match keyword for [solar battery storage], Google might start to serve ads for [solar battery] or [battery storage], which are not the same thing at all. When this occurs, you need to add those search terms to a negative keyword list and keep marking them if they continue to appear. This exercise can be painstaking, but rest assured, eventually you will have a clean search result. The good news is that you only pay when someone clicks. As long as the customer does read your ad, chances are they won't click on something wildly off-topic from their intended search. But don't take shortcuts. Check your campaigns daily, looking at the search results, that is, what keyword phrases prompted your ad to be shown to make sure it's "pure." Much like Pandora, the second you stop thumbing down a song you don't like, the algorithm shifts and, before you know it, you're hearing music that is way outside of your desired genre. Be the master and control your destiny!

 ANNA'S TIP

Never advertise on your own business name unless a competitor is. That is one of the easiest ways to overspend. If no competitor is advertising your name and a customer comes to Google and searches for you, your organic website will pop up right at the top first organic position. If you are advertising on your name or don't have a negative keyword list with your company name in it, your expensive ad will appear right above your organic listing and 30 percent+ of people will click on the first thing they see, drastically impacting your budget and goals to acquire new customers. If an advertiser is bidding on your name, create a unique "brand protection campaign" and set a low CPC of $1 max. As this is your company, Google will most likely show you as the top result and then the competitors beneath you (before your organic listing).

To wrap up this topic, don't ever accept automatic changes from Google on your account, with the exception of removing redundant keywords. Don't cut corners. Manually review all recommendations and know that Google won't help you get any credits back on your account, even if you can prove that the keyword that was shown was not on your list or was a negative keyword. One final thing to mention is that while we reviewed GoogleAds settings, the same rules apply when building a Microsoft Ads campaign. That being said, always remember to never allow GoogleAds and Microsoft Ads to sync in real time (import one-time during campaign initial setup and then break the connection). Also note that the CPC in Microsoft should be no more than one-third the cost for those same keywords in Google.

There are other important platform nuances so please reference the *thecovertcode.com* extended resource section to ensure favorable results when extending search intent to include this platform.

 ANNA'S TIP

Front-load your marketing spend for launch. After your initial $1,500 spend, commit to another three weeks with search impression share over 50 percent on all campaigns to get a real view of your potential. Starting and stopping campaigns online result in the algorithms' learning process breaking. That means you are starting over again, so don't do that. Whatever your annual marketing budget is, go ahead and allocate 50 percent to search and stick with it, making optimizations to increase results.

01000011 011011
01101111 01100100 01100101 001000
001000
01101111 011001
01101111 01100100 011001
01101111 011001
01101111 01100110 00100000

CHAPTER EIGHT

GENTLE NUDGE (REMARKETING EXPLAINED)

Remarketing, believe it or not, was responsible for me getting a call that changed my life in 2017. The call was from Paul Sullivan,[9] who explained that he was in charge of SunPower's partner relations and was looking to increase their preferred vendors. I tried to temper my excitement. Just exactly how did my relatively small agency make it onto SunPower's radar?

What happened was that Paul had visited SolarTechnologies. com and, upon leaving, was followed all over the internet, courtesy of my aggressive remarketing campaign. Curious who was behind the marketing, he went back to the site, scrolled to the bottom, found my Powered by Covert Communication link, and clicked through to my

---

9   Watch the Podcast with Paul Sullivan live from RE+ 2023.

website. He poked around a bit and then left. I'm sure you can guess what happened next. He was seeing both Covert and Solar Technologies ads following him everywhere he went.

This shouldn't come as a surprise. We know that, in order to move our customer through the purchase funnel, we must show them enough messages (frequency) over a short period of time (reach). Remarketing or, as I lovingly refer to it, "cyber-stalking" offers advertisers the ability to target customers post-site-visit by following them wherever they go next on their online browsing session. The magic starts by placing a pixel (cookie) on your domain. Then, as website visitors arrive, we tag them and add them into an audience pool. Once they leave, we follow them through the display, social, or programmatic networks showing them ads as they browse/listen/watch, ensuring that they continue to be reminded about our brand and reach critical messaging impression share.

When it comes to media partners that offer remarketing, it's critical to have options and, as always, you must see it to believe it. So let's dive into the basics of account settings, audience funnels, bidding strategies, and how to pick the right partner to optimize your campaign for success.

HOW TO PLAY THE GAME

Today, every media publisher selling online solutions will offer and ask for your remarketing business. How to determine which company is right for you will depend on several factors: speed to launch, creative ability, bid and delivery strategy, reporting, support, and, of course, results. In some cases, you could choose to use multiple partners (we will run through an example further in this chapter). Regardless of your decision, never put all your eggs in one basket. With so much money on the table from driving qualified paid search to your website, days without remarketing can drastically impact your campaign's results. It is for this reason that I always pixel my client websites with *at least* two reputable providers. If, for any reason, one campaign stops working because of a technical error or billing issue, or results start to diminish, we can pivot quickly to the other platform. How you will pick the right players starts by understanding how remarketing ads can be delivered and optimized.

CAMPAIGN SETTINGS

Just like with other online tools, the first step is to pick your ad campaign strategy. Depending on your industry or how long you have been running your online marketing, your strategy can and will change over time and in step with seasonal factors.

The top strategies include:

- *Awareness and Engagement:* This strategy is focused on increasing impression share and generating website traffic to your site. It will speed up impression delivery and attempt to serve ads as fast as possible to all users in your audience pool.

- *Conversion:* This strategy is focused on targeting impressions to those visitors that have the highest likelihood of converting into a hard goal or transaction. This strategy limits impression share to all visitors and instead focuses efforts on those users that we believe, through their online behavior, will have the highest likelihood of converting. A target goal of COS (cost of sales) or a solid CPA target spend per conversion can also be added, depending on which partner you use. Just like with search, these targets are a goal and not promised; they also might limit your impression share ability, so leave them blank. We will figure out what these numbers are from actual data, not wishful thinking.

- *Revenue:* Some platforms offer this as a unique strategy. It is focused on getting users to buy more while visiting your site. Stay away from strategy unless you are a large retailer commanding thousands of daily visits and are using unique upsell strategies and sales funnels.

FREQUENCY CAPPING AND PACE

Next, you will have the opportunity to pick how many ads you wish to serve to a user over a period of time. This directly relates to your budget and bid strategy, but my recommendation is to not set a frequency cap (our mission is to get our ad shown as many times as possible), but DO pace ads to distribute (optimize) evenly over your campaign period (i.e., monthly max budget), and then weekly target with daily spend caps. There may be reasons why you would want to accelerate impression share rapidly, but we'll get to that.

TARGETING OPTIONS

Depending on the platform, you will have options to narrow your ad delivery based on devices, operating systems, and environment. This includes options to target users across specific devices—desktops and laptops, tables, phones—or by mobile operating systems, such as Android of IOS, as well as through environments that those devices use to access inventory supply types online, including web and app (users online and within applications), web only, or in-app only. Although it might seem appealing to use all targeting options, I recommend only using "web" and leaving in-app out of the picture. In my experience, including in-app targeting results in unfavorable results and excessive bounce rates. Think about how annoying it is when you're playing the free version of Words with Friends when a pop-up ad flashes on the screen. More times than not, users accidentality click on the ads, resulting in high bounce and poor results.

Next, you will select your geolocation by country, state, region, or zip code (just like search, you do not want to spend impression share on visitors to your site unless they are physically located in an area you service). There will also be options to restrict types of sites or topics that you do not wish your ads to run on, that is, political, religious, medical. You can also upload a domain list to further guarantee that your ads will not be shown on unwanted domains.

There are additional targeting options, such as keyword lists or contextual targeting, meaning that we want to curate impression delivery in favor of sites that focus on a type of topic (auto, entertainment, etc.). My recommendation is to stick with the basics and don't limit yourself. Remember that your goal is to target everyone who comes to your website with as many messages as you can to build up the critical mass and then determine how long was the average customer path from first visit to conversion, how many ads they needed to see before they converted, and where that first_visitor originated from before converting, so you can clearly identify online opportunity and shift more digital budget in favor of those higher-quality paid sources.

AUDIENCE FUNNELS

The next critical factor is audience targeting based on length of time from the user's last visit to your website. The standard targeting is zero to thirty days; you can also decide how many visits that user needed to make to qualify them to be added into the audience pool. This number should always be set to one visit. We don't want to hope they come back a second time before we decide to serve them ads!

There are also other options that can limit your reach. For example, you could upload an exclusion list of existing customers. That might sound like a good idea, since you already have them. WRONG. Just because they are already a customer doesn't mean that they don't need to be constantly reminded about why they are. It's also a big mistake to stop serving ads to those who result in a "conversation" because, as we know, the sales process can take a long time. Once we get the lead, we must double down and make sure they stay engaged. Treat all site visitors the same. What's important is to focus on how long it's been since that customer visited your site, and then, as time goes by, adjust expectations and bids. You don't need to be as aggressive with impression share as time decays. The first seven to ten days are the most important to win impression share and get up to critical mass messaging (remember your funnel!).

Now, when it comes to building audience pools, you can and should create different benchmarks based on your industry type that help answer these questions: 1. How long does my average customer take from demo to contact signed? 2. What is this customer worth to my business?

The purpose of remarketing funnels is to place audiences into targeted buckets (audience pools) so you have the ability to change your bid strategy, as well as creative, depending on how long it has been since they last visited your website.

- *Lower Funnel:* Typically zero to thirty days, but I like to create more opportunities to learn and scale efforts, so I also create a zero- to seven-day and eight- to thirty-day in addition to the regular zero- to thirty-day audience pools.

- *Middle Funnel:* Thirty-one to sixty days or could be broken down deeper into thirty-one to forty-five days or forty-five to sixty days, depending on your industry and trends.

- *Upper Funnel:* Get ready, because I'm going to say something controversial: We *can* target a customer for up to four hundred days. I know that some of you are rolling your eyes. Four hundred days? Why on earth would we do that? Well, the easy answer is that sometimes it takes a long time to convert traffic, especially as related to the tourism industry. For example, here in Hawaii, it's typical that families will start the research phase a full year before they set foot in the islands. During this "intent" phase of their purchase funnel, they look at activities, hotels, the price for flights, hikes, and try to pick an island. Assuming that the customer does not clear their cache (which most don't), that would allow me, the advertiser, to sit dormant on their computer, monitoring online behavior. Once the customer starts to show interest again in Hawaii, boom, I'm showing them ads. No, we don't serve impressions at the same frequency, bid the same, or even show the same creative, as they slip further away from the last visit. I rarely use the long-tail upper funnel, but do recommend a sixty- to ninety-day and 90- to 120-day audience pool, which can prove to be useful for those companies that have extended sales funnels. This also is more probable now with many sites expiring cookie sessions after inactivity as we learned in chapter 6.

Another important topic to mention again is the "cookieless" movement that will directly impact advertisers' ability to store user data via cookie, but don't worry too much as the partners mentioned in the following pages have solutions in place to aid advertisers and the most important part about remarketing is using first-party cookies (our real site traffic) not third-party cookies (which are being deprecated for security and other consumer protection reasons).

BIDDING

The industry standard for remarketing bidding across media publishers is by CPM, but I always prefer to pay by CPC, which I find to be the most cost-effective and easiest to control. Did you know that two-thirds of all website visitors do not click on ads but rather will return organically to your site and convert after viewing an ad? Just like all online media, the game is the same. We want to create urgency with our media publishers and dangle a carrot so that they serve our ads more frequently, building impression share while controlling our costs by only agreeing to pay when a customer clicks. Just like starting your first search campaign, I recommend focusing on awareness as your primary strategy, and then, when you have enough conversion data (a couple hundred), you can switch and focus on conversions if you're happy with the results.

KEY REPORTING METRICS

Depending on the platform, you may have different data points, but the most important are:

- *Audience size*—how many people do we have the opportunity to serve ads.
- *Exposed users*—how many of those in our audience pool have we been able to serve an ad.
- *Displays*—how many total impressions did we serve and the CPM (or eCPM) cost to serve them.

- *Clicks*—how many clicks we generated and at what CPC cost, as well as the CTR to determine, out of all the ads we served, what percentage clicked. In search, we target for a minimum of 7 percent CTR; with remarketing, we're happy with 0.4–1 percent.

- *Frequency*—average number of times a user saw our ad, over the period of the campaign or, when possible, daily.

- *Win Rate*—number of displays divided by the total number of display opportunities. That metric is only offered in Criteo currently (from my list of vendors below). It essentially means that, out of all the available inventory, how many of them did you win, resulting in an impression being delivered. Remember that the ad exchange is a live auction happening in real time. As the customer scrolls down the page, ads will be won based on how many other advertisers are trying to reach the same users, and how much they are willing to spend to win that display opportunity. If you have a low win rate, that means that your bid was not high enough, but it can also indicate which scroll on the page your ad was shown. Think about it the same way as search ad position: Google could show your ad in eight possible places on the first page of results, and remarketing works the same way, but is based on how many scrolls the customers make down the page. On each scroll, new display inventory opens up and everyone on the exchange is bidding for the opportunity to serve an ad to that visitor.

- *Conversions*—for those with shopping carts, this number will show your number of sales and can also calculate total revenue and average cart value. For non-retail, this would include hard conversions that you have indicated via tag manager to fire as trackable events. Remember, your remarketing attribution should be twenty-four-hour view-through and thirty-day click conversion to appropriately give credit to your remarketing campaign. The view-through will be seen *inside* of your remarketing platform partner, and only clicks can be verified in G4 (remember that G4 won't be able to know if a customer saw your ad and then came back organically and converted, but they will see the click-to-convert traffic). Don't forget to use a unique UTM on every ad creative to make sure you know what's working and appropriately assign source credit.

AD CREATIVE AND DISPLAY TARGETING

The most effective remarketing is cross-platform, which means that we can target visitors through various ad exchange suppliers' inventory. Depending on the platform we pick, that can extend beyond the traditional display to include native, pre-roll video, CTV, audio, in-game, and social. To maximize your results, you want to make sure to use all ad sizes at your disposal (these vary by publisher, but always use all available sizes they offer). Most advertisers only use ten of the most popular banner ad sizes: 300px × 250px, 150px × 72px, etc. However, the ad exchange currently offers thirty-five banner sizes and growing. Each time a new device comes out with a unique screen size, or companies press the bounds of web design, new opportunities present themselves in terms of available content space.

With regard to remarketing, creative is fairly easy to test as the platform will be able to determine, after enough impressions are served, which creative and ad sizes performed better, and then optimize to deliver those more frequently on your behalf.

ANNA'S TIP

Always select the setting "optimize" that allows the remarketing platform to test and choose the ad that delivers higher performance. There are other ways to control ad delivery, including options to rotate ads, run ads in sequence (based on number of displays each user sees before switching creative), or prioritize delivery.

My recommendation is to design two sets of creative and let them run at the same time for the first sixty to ninety days of your campaign (depending on the amount of traffic you generate). It's also enjoyable for the customer to see variations of your ad so they don't get bored, and then you can determine if one was the clear winner or maybe, depending on the results, you could choose to show the better set (higher CTR) to lower funnel audiences, and then switch the creative when they reach another milestone, such as moving from lower to middle. There are different options in terms of creative display types, including static image, dynamic (animated ads), showcase (these pull directly from a shopping cart or product feed), or video. You can also choose where to serve your ad from, meaning the location where these assets are hosted (within the platform or on another server). This goes back to the concept of proof of delivery from chapter 5. Some partners will allow creative to be hosted externally using HTML Ad Tags or VAST/VPAID tags for hosting external video, but not all do (we don't trust those guys).

For retailers or companies with product feeds like real estate companies, a showcase ad is a clear must-do and is easy to integrate (just follow the platform instructions). This offers advertisers the ability to serve more relevant ads based on what the customer previously viewed or added to a shopping cart. It can also show them other similar products that they may not have seen, but might be interested in based on what they did engage with. Showcase ads also contain links taking the customer directly back to that listing/product post-click. I recommend that those using showcase ads also create a dynamic creative set featuring generic brand messaging. This is important because it will also allow you to cross-promote and support new product rollouts, promotions, events, big announcements, and keep your audience engaged. Just because they didn't come back and buy the item they previously looked at doesn't mean you can't win back another visit by showing them something new. The combination of showcase and display exposes customers to more reasons to shop while they continue to see products they already showed interest in or left in the cart—double win.

For those without product feeds, the recommended content type is dynamic, but you can also use static image ads if you have limited creative abilities (it's still a brand impression), and for those with engaging video, absolutely yes, it's worth uploading the three sizes available. Make that impact, baby!

Is your head spinning yet with all the opportunities to surprise and delight your customers? This is just the tip of the iceberg. Today, there are even ways to connect your CRMs' sales pipelines to create new audience pools, with unique creative messaging focused on helping those users move along the funnel faster. For example, you could show specific ads to help increase the likelihood that a lead will attend the seminar they signed up for, and then, after attending, change the creative to focus on testimonials or key features/solutions that will build confidence and increase the likelihood of them con-verting into a paid customer. Even post-sale, you could create a new audience pool and shift creative to upsell another service, or promote joining a referral program. The opportunities are endless!

As expected, depending on your industry, seasonality plays a key factor in how you will use funnels to maximize results. For example, with regard to solar, the peak season is Q2 and Q3, and then we see demand decrease the closer we move toward the holiday. At the same time, Q4 is the peak season for retailers, and they flood the exchange with aggressive budgets and bids to maximize holiday sales. Understanding seasonality is critical because you don't want to be spending more than you should, and as bids happen in real time, changing funnel targeting is one of the easiest ways to control your results. For your business's top season, utilize smaller funnels so you can make sure you win those critical first zero to seven and eight to thirty days of impression share. When it's off-season, change to focus on zero to thirty or zero to sixty days and drop your bids. Your win rate will go down but that's OK. You're still serving ads to customers on what I refer to as "the back of the funnel," meaning lower on the page scroll or deeper in the customer's journey. In my solar example, over the summer/fall I want to shoot for a 70–100+ percent win rate, while over the holiday I'm happy to win 30 percent of the time because I'm not interested in going up against retailers on a Christmas timeline. I'm in it for the long game.

For the retail industry, advertisers talk about the concept of time decay. Think about it like visiting the mall. Marketers know that, after seven days, the chances of you buying that dress or pair of pants drop dramatically. That's why retailers change the window display frequently, and smart stores will roll out new items slowly. Their goal is to make sure that weekly shoppers will come back to the store to see what's new, meanwhile buying an item they might not have committed to the previous week because they had a change of heart, or maybe this week it's on sale. If we can't get the shopper back in seven days, the likelihood declines with every day or week that passes. It's for this reason that I recommend, during retail peak seasons, to focus on showcase display for zero to seven days and then run generic branding from eight to fourteen days before dropping the customer out of the remarketing funnel. Remember, the next time they visit your site they will be replaced into the zero- to seven-day audience pool, and if you haven't been able to convince them after fourteen days, they most likely have picked another retailer and you should spend money on converting your new traffic. You can't win them all! Now that we know how the game works, let's talk about picking partners that you can trust.

For more detailed examples of how to build remarketing campaigns and case studies by partners using different platforms and strategies, visit the resource section at *thecovertcode.com*.

- *Criteo:* My preferred remarketing partner, based in France. Why they are my favorite is because they offer the ability to control bids manually by CPC (just like Google, they will recommend that you let them bid for you, but you know better: stay in control), and I *always* see my ads dominate in display. Some of the limitations of this partner are that a company cannot create their own account and support is unreliable. Sometimes it can take just a few days to create an account, other times it can take weeks or months (but worth the wait!). Another key difference is that they do not offer live chat (it's a bot), and unless you're using a showcase display (connected with product feed) you have to generate the creative yourself, which can place a cost burden on smaller companies, as they offer the most inventory with thirty-five ad sizes. A key benefit of Criteo is their pixel saturation, meaning that they have a lot of customers and media weight (cookied browsers out in the world) and can deliver ads faster and with greater bidding power than other publishers. They also provide detailed reports and metrics like win rate and exposed users, fake click credits, and delivery proof that impressions ran and on which domains.

- *AdRoll:* This company has been a trusted leader in the past, but over the last few years has slipped, resulting in higher costs and hard-to-control campaign results, making forecasting and predictive campaign spending unreliable. One of the benefits of AdRoll is that anyone can create an account and request free ads to run. Once the creative is uploaded, the campaign can be live within twenty-four to forty-eight hours and they offer wonderful live chat 24/7. My biggest concern with AdRoll is that you have no control over your bids and, although you can pick a bid strategy, the results are never in line with your desired threshold. For example, you might set your optimization to a desired CPM at $6 or CPC at $5 (considered aggressive), but the end results could be CPM of $60 and CPC of $75 and wildly unpredictable, meaning that even while running multiple campaigns, in the same industry, in the same target areas, I was not able to determine any trend in spending based on bid settings. Concerning indeed. My instinct is that, just like other platforms that use a daily budget, at the end of the day AdRoll will claim whatever budget you give them, no matter what, and that results in higher cost (CPM and CPC) to the advertiser and also indicates that AdRoll doesn't have the buying power it once did. When viewing bidding options, you will see a copy that essentially says that you can set a bid, but they'll do whatever they want: "If you specify a target, AdRoll will optimize your bids while treating the Target as an upper price-per-result not to exceed. However, it's possible that some Conversions, Clicks, or Impressions may exceed this target." AdRoll also offers cross-platform reach, including social (Facebook/Instagram, etc.), which used to be a favorable way to deliver trusted ads. All things considered, AdRoll is a great last resort and will get the job done (you will see ads), just keep it on the web display network and make this your first step and a temporary remarketing solution, as running ads will cost significantly more (3× at least in my experience) than through other highlighted platforms.

- *StackAdapt:* A relatively new partner for my agency, Stack-Adapt is Canadian based and has the best of both worlds in terms of bidding strategies and offers ways to remarket to customers across programmatic digital inventory beyond traditional display, including native, video, CTV, audio, and in-game. They also offer robust third-party oversight and the ability to create an image pixel that will run on your ad to double verify that your impressions were delivered. In order to create a campaign, companies must request a demo and then, depending on your company size, you might be invited to use the self-service platform or be asked to go with a managed account (they control) that includes a minimum spend. Over the short time I have used this solution, I have been very pleased with the accurate forecasting and delighted that reported results inside the platform matched G4.

- *Quantcast:* Truth be told, while using this platform since 2018 I have never "picked" them as my remarketing partner largely because of the high upfront cost to use the platform. Recently in November of 2023 I was invited to the "self-service" program allowing my clients to use this tool without a contract or high minimum ($10 per day requirement) so will be able to provide further insights into overall remarketing performance. That being said, when engaging in a front-funnel campaign using Quantcast, it's a mandate that you allow remarketing through this platform to increase the algorithm's learning and overall results. Currently Quantcast supports display, native, video, and CTV with plans to add blended in-game and audio in the future. As the industry evolves toward the cookieless movement, companies like Quantcast with trusted proprietary first-party data will become even more important to reach audiences at the moment of intent and reduce media waste by dropping those same users from targeting once they are "out of market."

 ANNA'S TIP

Always place at least two pixels for remarketing companies so that you can ensure that ads are being served. As AdRoll is easy to set up, start there while you go through the steps to get approved by Criteo and StackAdapt. Although these are vetted solutions, there are many other companies and they might provide similar value and oversight, so just make sure to use your Covert Code guidelines when selecting a partner.

To finish our thoughts on remarketing, business owners should never spend a penny on digital marketing or any marketing that drives traffic to your website without a robust remarketing program in place. Although there isn't a "critical mass" equation for success online, as previously mentioned my personal goal is to serve a customer four to seven banner ads per day for the first seven days after a customer's visit to a domain, OR at least twenty-one impressions by day 10, OR at a bare minimum thirty impressions over thirty days after visiting a client's website (and then maintain no less than a 30 percent win rate in low periods and a target of at least 70 percent for peak seasons). That being said, as we have learned, online is a moving target. What worked today will change tomorrow, and when it does, so will my media mix. Overall the mission is the same, we *must* stay relevant and top of mind with enough impressions to move the customer through the purchase funnel (*critical mass equation* minimum of four to seven messages over seven to ten days).

When using a media publisher (like Criteo) that does allow you to optimize based on CPC, it's worth noting that this can limit your audience reach. Why? Because the media partner is being paid when someone clicks and thus, they are going to serve ads to IPs that do click on ads more frequently than those that do not. They can determine that this specific user just isn't an ad clicker (or hover over ads showing intent), resulting in a portion of your audience that will never be exposed, and this number can swing dramatically, depending on factors like seasonal competitiveness, your bid, etc.

Now that you're an expert, what could you do to accomplish higher audience reach? Set up a zero- to seven-day awareness-focused campaign with a competitive CMP bid on StackAdapt. Then, create a zero- to ten- and eleven- to thirty-day funnels on Criteo with an attractive CPC and daily budget. Boom, the best of both worlds, results in the highest combined impression shares over the first seven to ten days of your campaign. The possibilities are endless! Don't stop there. As display inventory can be saturated with competition, think about extending your remarketing using programmatic targeting across digital audio messaging (podcast sponsorships, streaming, and digital radio) or by adding video pre-roll, CTV ads, blended in-game, or native. The more ways you can engage and build impression share with your active audience, the higher the likelihood of them returning to your site and converting.

 ANNA'S TIP

With regard to CPC bidding, when you first start a remarketing campaign, you will need an audience pool of at least one hundred users before ads really start to be served. Start with an aggressive bid (maybe $2) to dangle a carrot to the platform, urging them to serve as many ads as possible. Schedule daily reports that show your spend, win rate, and CPC and then, as with search, adjust your bid up or down to reach the desired win rate. Note: 1.0 percent means 100 percent, and 0.47 means 47 percent. It is possible to win over 100 percent; it depends on the number of scrolls. If you have a 200 percent or 300 percent win rate, that means you're winning ad display on the second and third scroll. In StackAdapt, the platform will suggest a CPM, so just stick with that, or if you want to be more aggressive, go up a dollar. Go get 'em, tiger!

Now readers, always remember that just because it worked before does not mean that it will work the same way, week-over-week, month-over-month, at least not all the time. You can't set and forget bids or strategies. If your results vary, think about what else might have influenced your campaign. Is it a political season? Is it a holiday? Did a big hurricane happen? Did interest rates go up again? Don't be discouraged. Adjust your audience funnels (smaller or larger pools), try a different strategy, change your bid and budget (dangle the carrot), and then see what happens. Remember, it's a game and sometimes you win and sometimes you lose. What's important is that you are learning and having fun! Now that we have tackled all the hard stuff, let's conclude with the popular topic of social media in our last chapter.

 ANNA'S TIP

For advertisers not physically located in the area you're trying to target, always add your zip code into the targeted list and make sure your browser is not blocking ads. Then visit your website often and make sure you are seeing ads. If you have been running for over a week and are seeing reported impressions or measurable daily per-user frequency and have not ever seen the ad yourself, then chances are you have the wrong partner. Want to see how it should work? Visit covertcommunication.com and enjoy! Remember, I'm only being charged if you click.

01000011 01101
01101111 01100100 01100101 001000
001000
01101111 011001
01101111 01100100 011001
01101111 011001
01101111 01100110 00100000

CHAPTER NINE

SOCIAL MEDIA

Social media is a topic that deserves a book all on its own. Over the past decade, it has been considered one of the most important tools to engage with consumers. But it can quickly become a money pit if companies don't set the correct expectations by platform, and fail to understand how to measure results.

When evaluating social media channels and creating a content and engagement strategy, it's critical to understand that they are just like other domains/apps and are considered content publishers with an active audience. Just like with search engines, social media strategies should be broken into two buckets: organic and paid. What companies must know is that engaging in any form of social strategy is a serious time commitment. Just because everyone else is doing it doesn't mean that it's going to return a measurable ROI. Depending on your brand's type and ability to utilize push versus pull marketing strategies, results can vary drastically and so must your company's expectations. "Pull" marketing means that your fans are creating content and championing your brand all on their own. They are pulling it down through social channels themselves. This reduces a company's social media investment by saving them time in content creation and costs associated with paid ads to reach their desired audience. "Push" marketing means that your brand must create urgency and spend more to generate the impression share that will influence the desired audience to participate and engage with your brand in a social space. Think about downloading a free copy of a new single from Britney Spears versus from Tool, a band that only comes out with a new album every decade (if that) and has fans anxiously awaiting to purchase. No discount or freebies required.

Another topic that always comes up with clients is the idea of virality. Everyone wants to "go viral," but as a marketing strategy, it doesn't add up because it's not guaranteed. I remember telling a client who was consumed with this concept, "What if I told you we were going to spend $30,000 and hope for a miracle?" That doesn't sound like a very good business decision, right? That's what "going viral" is, a pipe dream, and even for those that do find themselves trending at this level, the hype doesn't last long. You might have experienced a big boost in sales for a product or fan growth, but it's short-lived and not a long-term strategy that continues to build brand value or recurring revenue.

WHEN TO ENGAGE IN SOCIAL MEDIA

If your company is going to participate in social media activities, the first step is to weigh the opportunity costs. Effective social media means that your company will be posting meaningful and relevant content two to three times per week across key platforms like Facebook, Instagram, Google My Business, LinkedIn, Nextdoor,

Pinterest, TikTok, Threads, X, etc. It also means that you will be engaging with users in a two-way dialogue, and responding to their posts and messages in a timely and respectful manner—as a human, not using auto replies, and no less than twenty-four hours later. Effective social engagement also includes engaging with other businesses/brands, which includes tagging them and sharing and commenting on their content. It's important to recognize that you can't control customers' feelings or choice of words. I'll never forget when I was helping a hospice nonprofit organize a charity scavenger hunt called "Hot Pursuit." The director told me that we needed to make sure that the word "death" didn't appear on our social media. I had to explain that we couldn't control what people posted. If that was a concern, then adding Twitter hashtags into the signage was not recommended.

I often explain the evolution of media consumption to clients in terms of one-way versus two-way communication. Before the birth of social media and online review services, the media and companies spoke in one direction to the consumer. Messages were carefully crafted, controlled, and distributed. If a customer had a complaint, the only option was to write a letter. Today, communication is two-way. Customers have a voice and opportunities to speak directly back to the media and companies. This presents a tremendous opportunity to create lifelong relationships, but comes with more risks than rewards when not managed in the correct way. It's also important to mention that this type of communication means that conversations are *never* private and largely uncontrolled.

ANNA'S TIP

Social media is an opportunity to engage with your audience in a two-way conversation. If you don't want to commit to this, then pick another way to control your messaging. Remember, even with a paid social media, the end users can still make comments that are public and seen by all other people your ad is reaching.

When to Use Social Media

- Create an engaged audience
- Increase share of mind
- Increase customer loyalty
- Increase referrals and social vitality
- Drive website traffic
- Drive measurable sales (for retailers)
- Increase off-site SEO link building
- Influence behavior
- *When Not to Use Social Media*
- Generate relevant content
- Engage with users in a timely or respectful manner
- Control how people will consume or engage with your content

LEARNING THE GAME

The goal of social media platforms is to grow subscribers and then command as much of their daily screen time as possible, that is, multiple daily sessions with a long average-per-session-time spent across devices like mobile, tablet, and computer. To do this, you need to curate content so that, during each session, users see the content that they care about and are not flooded with posts that aren't relevant, resulting in an exit. Too many bad sessions and the result? Potential customers stop coming altogether. They can't risk that.

You might be asking how social media platforms decide what to show in my feed? That all boils down to "engagement rates." In addition to the standard likes/hearts, watches, comments, and shares, this also includes "hovering" over a post. I refer to this as content that "stops the scroll." This indicates to the algorithm that a customer has interest, since they lingered over it for a couple of seconds versus scrolling right past it. These metrics add up as a score on your post, meaning that if your content was not "engaged" with enough by those subscribers who did see it, platforms will stop showing it on the feed.

The way I like to explain this conceptually to clients is that "you are only as good as your last post." As with a traditional blog or community message, each time you post content, it is added to the top of the page/board and old content with less relevant messages is hidden behind it (pushed lower on the feed). For example, if your dog was missing and you brought a sign into the coffee shop, chances are they would post that right in the middle of the board because it's important and people love dogs. If you came in again with a sign for a lemonade stand, it might not make the board, or might be tacked to the bottom or covered up quickly. There isn't enough space for all messages, and frankly, not everything is equal when it comes to content. This makes sense. With so many users, social platforms want to make sure that content creators spend more time creating thoughtful "stop the scroll" posts and are staying relevant with their fan base. Also, just because a subscriber liked "Ocean Vodka" last month doesn't mean they still want to see posts from them regularly; they might be interested in something else, like planning a home remodel or finding activities for an upcoming trip.

Based on what you are actively engaged with, social platforms curate your content feed to ensure that you are seeing a healthy mixture of friend, fan, and paid content during each active session. This same concept applies to personal accounts, meaning that if you don't like your friends/family content, you will stop seeing it. That also means that every post your company makes sets a new baseline on your account in terms of relevancy. If that post has no likes, comments, shares, hovers, or watches, then it will not be shown. The challenge is that, unless the post is shown, no one can engage with it. That's why we need to talk about paid social media strategy.

When determining your social media strategy, there are some key metrics to consider:

- *Engagement*—This includes the number of followers/fans, comments, shares, likes, saves, clicks, watches, "views," and direct messages.
- *Virality rate/amplification rate*—These metrics show what percentage of your impressions are resulting in content spreading. This is calculated by the post shares divided by the impressions multiplied by one hundred to get the variety rate percentage.
- *Ad Metrics*—Similar to other forms of online paid sources, this includes total audience size, "reach" of your ads' impressions to those in the total audience, the number of impressions, CPM, clicks, CPC, CTR, and total conversions. For those running video ads, this also includes views and completion rates.
- *Customer Service Metrics*—There are other deeper types of social metrics that can be collected and reported, including average response time (customer message to company reply), share of voice, and social sentiment. These customer service metrics are commonly used by large corporations with significant market penetration (lots of company mentions and

hashtags) and "media weight," and can also be tied into types of customer satisfaction scores (CSAT) or Net Promoter Score (NPS), which are collected by sending a customer a survey (text, email, direct message).

TYPES OF SOCIAL CONTENT

When deciding which social media platforms to support, content formats are a key consideration. If you are using social media to build off-site SEO and rank, then it's critical that they support links within the body of the post. For example, Facebook, LinkedIn, X, and Google My Business do accept links in organic posts. With Pinterest, the post is the link (high SEO value and direct correlation to sales), unlike Instagram and TikTok, which offer links from bios or from paid ads, that is, little off-site value. Popular social content types include text, image, video, emojis, hashtags, and live video streaming. For retailers, social media content can also include links to their product feed externally or internally within the platform to make purchases (Facebook Marketplace or TikTok Shop).

SOCIAL MEDIA GOALS

When determining your social media strategy, you must also consider what is really important to your company. For some businesses, having likes and followers is a priority. While these numbers might make us feel good, it doesn't mean that they will have an ROI or direct impact on sales. This concept is called "social proofing" and, for some industries like retail, we do see a correlation between number of followers and post-likes and paid advertising. Why? Because, when a customer is buying a product, it makes them feel more secure seeing that other people are positively engaged. This is not the case with other industries, but having more likes on your content can help you reach more people organically. This concept is referred to as your "active audience" and the more engagement each post has, the greater likelihood of it being shown to existing fans/followers.

Bottom line: If it's important to the business owner, it's important. But it should also match expectations, because to generate those user actions will require a paid subscription or ad campaign. Remember, social media platforms are a business and their goal is to monetize their subscribers and win media dollars from advertisers.

SOCIAL MEDIA BUDGETS

Should your organization decide to commit to content creation, it's recommended that you plan a budget for "boosting" content to your existing fans and "friends of fans." This will ensure that your content reaches people whom you care about and also will generate the largest amount of engagement on that content. By leveraging the power of the friend effect ("Oh, Jocelyn likes Ocean Vodka. I think she is cool so I'm going to like them too. I don't want to miss out"), we can hopefully grow fans/followers at the same time without a separate budget focused on "growing fans": a double win.

When creating paid ads, note that each platform has different options. In Meta, there is no engagement forecast or ability to set a target CPC or CPM after you build a campaign. This makes it very hard to estimate results or plan for traffic lift, as it swings so rapidly.

To create the best opportunity for your campaign to drive traffic and sales, always set a lifetime budget of thirty days so that the algorithm has enough time to "find the match" and serve enough impressions to those users. If you set a short time frame, what ends up happening is that Meta (or other social media platforms) will spend all your money no matter what, resulting in poor performance. For example, let's say our business wants to promote a seminar for exit planning in Chicago that is happening in five days. After we build our campaign in Facebook, we might learn that our potential reach is 10,000 people and we decide to spend $100 per day over the next five days. At the end of the campaign, we might have only served 2,000 impressions, but Facebook will still claim all the funds. The longer the algorithm has to run, the easier it is to find those desired users and serve them impressions. The platform wants to do its best, but the shorter the time they have, the harder it is. It also depends on how many sessions that desired target user has, as well as what other advertisers are bidding on the same eyeballs. Overall, this can dramatically swing your CPM or CPC results from campaign to campaign.

In my experience, the only social media ads that really return valuable ROI are for retailers attached to a shopping cart. This shouldn't come as a surprise at this point to any reader. A transaction is easy to track, a lead is not. Plus, with so many millions of transactional conventions, social channels like Meta/TikTok are very good at positioning your product to users with the greatest likelihood to buy based on all their real-time data points. When setting budgets for most small- to medium-sized companies, my recommendation is to start small with a $500 budget (narrow your targeting to focus on your fans and "friends of fans") and run the campaign for a month. Review results. Then run the same campaign again and see if you can establish a baseline for COS, average cart price, and total revenue. Once the algorithm has enough conversions, it's pretty easy to trust, but it is risky to try and "dangle a carrot" in this medium, so set a long lifetime budget and, after you have three months of solid trending data (similar results), try and increase by $250 to see if that results in more sales or just a higher price-per-result before attempting to shift media funds or expanding your target audience. For non-retailers, you may want to explore other options. With the growth of programmatic advertising, there are plenty of other places you can spend your hard-earned money and generate higher-quality traffic with a lower cost-per-lead. You can always set a small $300 budget to boost posts ($10 per) and engage a social proofing service like We Just Social (https://wejustsocial.com/) to boost followers and likes on Instagram at a low cost per month and call it a day.

 ANNA'S TIP

Always create long-tail lifetime ads in social channels (thirty days) and give the platform time to deliver the best results and "make the match." The shorter the campaign length the higher the cost to deliver impressions and generate clicks.

Before I end this chapter, I want to share a few final thoughts on social media. Although this feels like a must-do for all businesses, times are changing. With the increase in AI and growing mistrust online, many users just don't feel the same way as they once did about this form of communication. It is OK to not engage in social media, and if you have little time or resources to commit, the better place to focus company efforts is on brand reputation management and growing positive reviews on Google My Business, which has a direct and meaningful impact on your off-site SEO, can decrease your CPC in SEM, all while building consumer confidence online. A triple win! For more on brand reputation management risks and rewards, visit our resource section.

01000011 011011
01101111 01100100 01100101 001000
001000
01101111 011001
01101111 01100100 011001
01101111 011001
01101111 01100110 00100000

CONCLUSION

Stop, Drop, and Roll. That was a saying that was burned into our heads as children (pun intended), but it worked and saved countless lives. It wasn't silly. It was witty and something that humans needed to break through the panic and to silence the noise with a solution. Rather than screaming for help and flapping our arms around, we were armed and empowered.

Right now, that is exactly what companies need to navigate the rapidly evolving world of digital advertising. The reality is that, in pixels, there is no discrimination based on race, gender, or age. Everyone is at risk, and most are being straight-up bamboozled. Why? Because it's just so easy to be a con man online. Someone can show you data and tell you what it means, and you will believe it. Some of what is said may be the truth, or it might all be fabricated, but how can you tell the difference? Many times, they're lies that are being told that then become "truths" that are recited and resold. The cost can be measured in billions of dollars lost to digital fraud, bankruptcy, and corporate theft.

The devastation is widespread and growing, crippling businesses of all sizes as online marketing becomes the largest part of the media mix and is viewed as the most effective way to target audiences at the lowest cost, reducing the noise, clutter, and wasteful spending that impacts a customer's time and a business's bottom line.

The truth is that online advertising *can* be the holy grail when managed wisely and strategically, when the rules are learned, practiced, and applied. And the good news is that everyone is capable of learning how digital marketing works.

I've kept this goal—to equip readers with knowledge and tools— at the top of my mind as I wrote this book. In this rapidly changing landscape, the right knowledge and the right tools are mission critical. There are so many factors that contribute to a customer's online experience, from the devices they use to the media outlets they trust, from world events to customer preferences. Every detail matters when you want to increase your ability to generate and convert website traffic from a click to a sale.

Now that you are armed with *The Covert Code*, you have the power to stay in control. This means that you will never "set and forget" bid strategies or trust others to make these critical decisions on your behalf. To be successful today, business owners must continue to evaluate their digital strategy and utilize the tools available to them to identify and curate customer relationships across online platforms. The bottom line is that you must always be on the lookout for fraud, including partnerships and reporting. When the numbers don't add up, you should be ready to pivot quickly. Don't be afraid to push the pause button and reassess your options.

With the advent and acceleration of AI, the need to understand how your business fits into a digital future is even more critical. What many fail to see is that, just like when social media was first introduced, AI is in its adoption phase with the goal to increase active subscribers. It's essentially free, or very low cost, but that won't last forever.

The same strategies I've shared throughout the book can help you with this and all the technology disruptions to come. Start by asking yourself whether the business choices you are making today are sustainable with so many unknowns. What might seem like a cost-saving strategy might quickly become a bottleneck and result in you knowing even less about your customer's journey, or lock you into technology decisions that will increase your cost-per-lead, cost-per-sit, and cost-per-sale long term. As we've discussed, be flexible and ready to explore new options, while arming yourself with best practices that will allow you to reach business goals today while positioning your brand to achieve the growth of tomorrow.

You're not alone. This is only the beginning of your journey into the exciting world of digital marketing. As you start to implement these best practices and evaluate your results, new opportunities to meet and exceed your business goals will open up to you. Believe in yourself and trust your instincts. You've got this!

What's next? Join us online for additional educational opportunities, including tutorials, podcasts, and forums. Sign up for our newsletter to stay in the know on all things related to mastering the art of digital media. Remember to check out the additional resources at *thecovertcode.com*.

And if you want to learn more about my work or my agency, or want to explore curated solutions for your business, contact me for real-change-consulting @ annacovert.com.

 ANNA'S TIP

Scan the QR code in the back of this book to get access to all of our preferred referral programs. Anyone who signs up using our link will help support a local Hawaii nonprofit. We also have negotiated special COVERT rates to help you get the very best solutions for your business.

```
01000011 01101111 01100100 01100101 00100000 01001101 01100001 01
01110010 01101001 01101110 01100111 00100000 01110100 01101000 01
01110010 01110100 00100000 01101111 01100110 00100000 01000100 01
01110100 01100001 01101100 00100000 01001101 01100001 01110010 01
01101001 01101110 01100111 01010100 01101000 01100101 00100000 010
01100101 01110010 01110100 00100000 01000011 01101111 01100100 01
01100001 01110011 01110100 01100101 01110010 01101001 01101110 01
01101000 01100101 00100000 01000001 01110010 01110100 00100000 01
01000100 01101001 01100111 01101001 01110100 01100001 01101100 00
01110010 01101011 01100101 01110100 01101001 01101110 01100111 010
00100000 01000011 01101111 01110110 01100101 01110010 01110100 00
01100100 01100101 00100000 01001101 01100001 01110011 01110100 01
01101110 01100111 00100000 01110100 01101000 01100101 00100000 01
00100000 01000011 01101111 01110110 01100101 01110010 01110100 00
01100100 01100101 00100000 01001101 01100001 01110011 01110100 01
01101110 01100111 00100000 01110100 01101000 01100101 00100000 01
00100000 01101111 01100110 00100000 01000100 01101001 01100111 01
01101100 00100000 01001101 01100001 01110010 01101011 01100101 01
01100111 01010100 01101000 01100101 00100000 01000011 01101111 01
01110100 00100000 01000011 01101111 01100100 01100101 00100000 010
01101111 01110110 01100101 01110010 01110100 00100000 01000011 01
00100000 01001101 01100001 01110011 01110100 01100101 01110010 01
00100000 01110100 01101000 01100101 00100000 01000001 01110010 01
01100110 00100000 01000100 01101001 01100111 01101001 01110100 01
01001101 01100001 01110010 01101011 01100101 01110100 01101001 01
01101000 01100101 00100000 01000011 01101111 01110110 01100101 01
01000011 01101111 01100100 01100101 00100000 01001101 01100001 01
01110010 01101001 01101110 01100111 00100000 01110100 01101000 01
01110010 01110100 00100000 01101111 01100110 00100000 01000100 01
01110100 01100001 01101100 00100000 01001101 01100001 01110010 01
01101001 01101110 01100111 01010100 01101000 01100101 00100000 010
01100101 01110010 01110100 00100000 01000011 01101111 01100100 01
01100001 01110011 01110100 01100101 01110010 01101001 01101110 01
01101000 01100101 00100000 01000001 01110010 01110100 00100000 01
01000100 01101001 01100111 01101001 01110100 01100001 01101100 00
01110010 01101011 01100101 01110100 01101001 01101110 01100111 01
00100000 01000011 01101111 01110110 01100101 01110010 01110100 00
01100100 01100101 00100000 01001101 01100001 01110011 01110100 01
01101110 01100111 00100000 01110100 01101000 01100101 00100000 010
00100000 01101111 01100110 00100000 01000100 01101001 01100111 01
01101100 00100000 01001101 01100001 01110010 01101011 01100101 01
01100111 01010100 01101000 01100101 00100000 01000011 01101111 01
01110100 00100000 01000011 01101111 01100100 01100101 00100000 01
01110100 01100101 01110010 01101001 01101110 01100111 00100000 01
```

01000011 0110111
01101111 01100100 01100101 0010000
0010000
01101111 0110011
01101111 01100100 0110010
01101111 0110011
01101111 01100110 00100000

GLOSSARY

BOUNCE RATE   The percentage of total website traffic that left your site immediately. This means that they did not "engage" in any way by scrolling their mouse down the page and hovering over page content.

CLICKS   A click on your ad

CDN   Content Delivery Network, often called Content Distribution Network, is a geographically distributed network of proxy servers and their data centers. These operators are used to deliver content to end users through internet service providers.

CPC   Cost-per-click generated from paid media

CPM   Cost to advertise 1,000 impressions

DEMAND-SIDE PLATFORM (DSP)   Demand-Side Platforms allow advertisers to buy ad space at the lowest cost possible and typically utilize AI. Supply-Side Platforms are for publishers to sell ad space.

DIRECT TRAFFIC
The user typed into their search browser your exact URL. They know you by name and have bookmarked your site. This number can commonly be high for companies that use their company site as the "homepage" for search engines, meaning that when an employee starts an online session, the company website page loads on a tab. To remove this type of data, a filter can be added into GoogleAnalytics. Users who are masking their IP will also appear as direct traffic, which means we do not know how they got to your domain (unknown path).

DOOH
Digital Out-Of-Home Ads

ECPCL
Cost-per-completed-listen

EMAIL TRAFFIC
The user clicked on a link inside of an email campaign. Email traffic can often be lumped into referral traffic if not appropriately tagged using a UTM parameter.

FREQUENCY
The number of times ads are shown over a period.

GEOTARGETING
Targeting users based on their physical location by country, state, city, zip/postal code, and radius levels. Radius can be defined by the latitude, longitude, and radius target around an area's address. For in-app, this can provide accuracy up to 10 m, but note that for such a small radius, scale may be severely affected, and the platform may not collect any users. Desktop and Mobile Web targeting under 3 km may be less precise.

IMPRESSION
A view of your ad online. CPM means the cost to deliver 1,000 impressions to your target audience.

IMPRESSION MULTIPLIER
Impression Multiplier or a one-to-many channel type means that the publisher is charging a specific number of impressions based on your DOOH ad location as many people will see it at the same time.

INVALID TRAFFIC (IVT)
Invalid traffic is an artificial rise in ad clicks and impressions on a website. It's mostly generated by automated software a.k.a. bot traffic. Fake!

MEDIA PUBLISHER Media publishers are sellers of online inventory spaces like website owners, app developers, social media platforms, and video streaming services and are typically the CDN (content delivery networks). Companies like Google, Criteo, Quantcast, and AdRoll are all types of media publishers.

ORGANIC TRAFFIC The user searched for your company by name or your company appeared in free search results from a customer's search for a product or service. This is earned traffic or free versus paid.

OTHER TRAFFIC Traffic that does not have a clear path or tracking code to identify how the user arrived at your website.

PAID TRAFFIC Traffic generated from some advertising campaigns on the ad exchange or search platform.

PROGRAMMATIC Programmatic advertising uses precise targeting to segment audiences with real data and automates the process of buying and selling data-targeted media across websites, apps, or venues with targeting factors like location, time of day, and weather.

REACH The number of viewers within a campaign flight date who were exposed to the ad.

REFERRAL TRAFFIC The user clicked on a link on a partner site to your site, essentially referring that session to your domain.

REMARKETING Remarketing (also retargeting) is a form of digital marketing that allows advertisers to pixel tag (cookie) a user who visits their website and then serve them digital ads after they leave the domain.

SITE EXIT Occurs after the user makes a successful land on your site and stays (not bounced). Site exit tracks the page they left from.

SOCIAL TRAFFIC The user clicked on a link within a social network like Meta, LinkedIn, etc., before arriving at your domain.

SUPPLY-SIDE PLATFORM (SSP)
Supply-side platform automates the selling of online media space by providing web publishers and DOOH media owners the ability to sell ad inventory at the highest price.

TIME OF DAY TARGETING
Targets users based on the time of day.

TRAFFIC SOURCE
Traffic sources indicate where your website traffic came from and are broken into direct traffic, organic, paid, social, referral, and unknown.

URCHIN TRACKING MODULE (UTM)
A way to track and measure the effectiveness of your online digital campaigns from all sources. UTMs are snippets of code that are placed at the end of your domain's URL that identify specific sources of traffic and campaign details.

VENUE TYPE TARGETING
Venue type targeting refers to where the digital ads are shown physically, that is, billboard, taxi top, in the mall, retailer, etc.

WEATHER TARGETING
Targets users based on weather.

01000011 0110111
01101111 01100100 01100101 0010000
0010000
01101111 0110011
01101111 01100100 0110010
01101111 0110011
01101111 01100110 00100000

CONTACT

Anna Covert is an unstoppable force in marketing and recognized as an authority in all things digital. Passionate about spreading the word on best practices in online and digital marketing, she is available for speaking engagements on topics related to this book and enterprise technology consulting services at annacovert.com

Services that Anna and her companies provide include:

Covert Communication—Integrated Marketing. Helping brands extend their traditional marketing efforts online, providing innovative, results-driven, integrated digital solutions.

Trusting Solar Calculator (Solar Wizard)—Solar calculator app that provides estimates of solar costs and savings for residential and commercial companies. Completely customizable, multi-languages, currently being used in over twenty-four countries.

Aerial Impacts—Customized direct mail company focused on home services to provide customized variable printed post cards to homeowners showing their home with solar on the roof, or other "like" services to increase quality leads.

Reatium.io—An open-source web platform that offers full stack technology services.

MANA—Software to save time and money. In Hawaiian MANA means power. The mission is to connect application programming interfaces through custom code without the use of Zapier or third-party services.

Anna can be reached at anna@covertcommunication.com, on LinkedIn, or through any of her websites.